OFFICE FOR STANDARDS
IN EDUCATION

Recent Research on Gender and Educational Performance

Madeleine Arnot
John Gray
Mary James
Jean Rudduck
with
Gerard Duveen
UNIVERSITY OF CAMBRIDGE
SCHOOL OF EDUCATION &
HOMERTON COLLEGE

...ONERY OFFICE

Office for Standards in Education
Alexandra House
33 Kingsway
London WC2B 6SE

Telephone 0171-421 6800

ISBN 0 11 350102 1

CONTENTS

LIST OF FIGURES AND TABLES

ACKNOWLEDGEMENTS

We would like to thank numerous colleagues, in this country and further afield, for their interest, advice and copies of research reports and papers to inform our thinking.

We are also grateful to many teachers and local inspectors for the information they made available and the accounts of practice that they offered, in writing and in discussion. We took heart from the knowledge that so many people, despite competing pressures on time and resources, were committed to exploring issues of gender, equity and achievement in their own settings.

We are grateful to Evelyn Arizpe for her help on gender and literacy and to Delyse Silverstone for collecting documentary evidence from schools. Their work on the bibliography has been invaluable. Alan Russell also deserves our gratitude for the tireless energy and patience he showed in helping us put together this report.

We were, throughout the study, appreciative of the support and advice offered by Oona Stannard HMI, Christine Agambar HMI, Head of the Research, Analysis and International team and David Read, Research Manager at OFSTED.

It has not been easy, within the confines of a short report, to achieve coverage and coherence – and to accommodate our own varied perspectives. For the shortfalls and omissions we offer a collective apology.

Cambridge
June 1998

INTRODUCTION

The Context

Over the last 20 years the gender issues that have shaped thinking and practice in schools have changed dramatically. In the 1970s and 80s, schools were responding to evidence of the patterns of girls' achievement while in the 1990s, they are responding to widely publicised statements about boys' underachievement.

There is concern in the UK and in other countries that the supposed superior achievement of girls may be used as an argument that there is no longer a need to focus on their education and that effort, therefore, needs to be put exclusively into work with and on boys. The issues surrounding boys' achievement are real and should not be underestimated but the question of gender and performance is more complex, affecting different sub-groups of boys and girls in different ways and often reflecting the influence of class and ethnicity.

This report, despite its inevitable limitations, aims to extend enquiry and debate. It demonstrates, like *The Gender Divide* (OFSTED/EOC, 1996) before it , that those seriously committed to raising standards and improving achievement for all pupils need to address issues of gender in looking for ways forward.

Scope of the Review

Given the volume of research on gender and education across different countries, different cultures and different educational systems, the review had to be selective. It concentrates mainly on research undertaken after 1988 (the year which saw the introduction of the GCSE as well as the National Curriculum and new assessment procedures). It also illustrates the now widespread commitment in schools, particularly as part of whole-school policy frameworks, to understanding how gender works in the local context and what strategies need to be developed to strengthen the achievement and life chances of all pupils.

The review underlines the significance, for understanding the patterns of young people's aspirations and achievement, of the interplay of issues of gender and issues of ethnicity, class and locality. By presenting the debate in terms merely of boys' and girls' performance, the complex reality of young people's worlds is over-simplified.

Performance, broadly defined, should go beyond the common criteria of examination passes and should cover the education of the whole child; however, we have been pragmatic in reflecting the definitions that have currency in the field – and these tend, on the whole, to be concentrated on achievement in tests and examinations. Because of constraints on space, the report indicates rather than develops the broader interpretations.

Structure of the Report

The report is organised in five parts. Part 1 offers a statistical summary of the evidence on gender and performance (focusing on young people between the ages of five and 18) and highlights the extent of similarities and differences in male and female achievement. Parts 2 and 3 consider various educational and social explanations for the patterns of pupil performance. Part 2 reviews the evidence concerning differences in pupils' approaches to learning and the effects of teaching and assessment styles in particular subjects and across the curriculum. Studies of the similarities and differences in performance of single sex and co-educational schools and the effectiveness of schools in closing the gender gap are also reassessed. Part 3 describes the different ways in which societal influences can affect school life and pupil reponses to educational success. Evidence is drawn from a range of studies of pupil motivation, peer group cultures and societal identities which highlight, for example, the significance of self-esteem, gender values and teachers' expectations of pupils, and the influence of the changes in the labour market and the family on young people in schools today. Many of these external influences which are drawn into the school from its social context have different effects on different groups of male and female pupils. Part 4 describes the ways in which small-scale research and developmental activities have been carried out in schools to improve gender performance patterns over the last 20 years. Part 5 offers a brief commentary on the implications of the review findings for national, local and institutional policy and practice.

PART 1

THE SIZE AND NATURE OF THE GENDER GAP

1 SIMILARITIES AND DIFFERENCES IN EDUCATIONAL PERFORMANCE

The traditional criterion for monitoring the school system has been the proportion of students securing five or more A* to C grades in public examinations at 16-plus. Since the late 1980s this figure has been rising steadily. At the same time the 'gap' in the performance of boys and girls appears to have been widening. This chapter first attempts to establish the extent to which gaps in performance between boys and girls are already evident amongst younger age-groups. It then considers performance at 16-plus in greater detail and the nature of gender disparities at A-level.

1.1 THE KEY STAGE EVIDENCE

National testing and assessment provide a comprehensive account of the attainments of boys and girls at the various Key Stages and in some of the subjects of the National Curriculum.

The pattern of performance in Reading or English at Key Stage 1 in 1995 seems pretty clear-cut. Girls made a better start at learning to read than boys; 83% of seven-year-old girls were performing at the 'expected level' (level 2) or above compared with 73% of boys (see Figure 1.1). Furthermore, 39% of seven-year-old girls reached level 3 or above compared with only 28% of boys (see Table 1.1a). The position is similar if one looks at any of the other components of English which were tested or assessed at the same time: writing, spelling, handwriting, and speaking and listening. Girls always out-performed boys and usually by a considerable margin.[1]

At Key Stage 2, 56% of 11-year-old girls reached level 4 (the expected level for this age-group) or above on the English test compared with 42% of boys; whilst at Key Stage 3, 26% of 14-year-old girls reached level 6 or above compared with only 14% of boys. Teachers' assessments of pupils sometimes produced even stronger patterns of differences.[2]

- Girls get off to a better start in Reading than boys; the lead they have established by Key Stage 1 is maintained at Key Stages 2 and 3.

Figure 1.1

Percentage of pupils at Key Stage 1 reaching 'expected level' (level 2 or above) in national assessments of Reading, Mathematics and Science

% of pupils

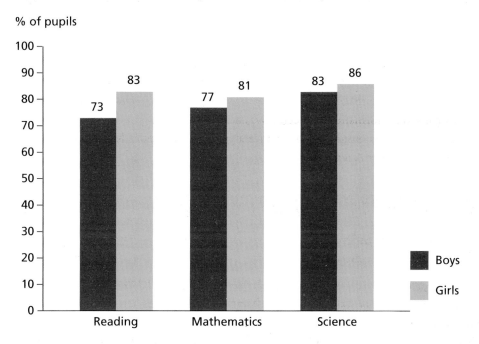

One needs to remember, of course, that the 1995 results provide three separate snapshots relating to three different age-groups and that a longitudinal study which followed the *same* pupils through the various Key Stages might provide a somewhat different picture. It seems unlikely, however, that the basic picture would change very much.

The picture in Mathematics is by no means so obvious. In 1995 81% of girls reached the 'expected level' or above at Key Stage 1 compared with 77% of boys (see Figure 1.1), whilst 18% of girls performed at level 3 or above on the Mathematics number test compared with 21% of boys. Teachers' assessments in the sub-areas of using and applying mathematics, number, algebra, shape and space, and handling data produced similarly small differences. By Key Stage 2, however, the differences had evened out. Forty-five per cent of girls scored at level 4 or above on the tests as did 44% of boys, although teachers' assessments had the girls a little further ahead. A similar picture is provided by the Key Stage 3 test results where the proportions getting level 6 or above were again very similar (33% of girls and 34% of boys) with teachers' assessments providing the same story.

Table 1.1

Performance in English, Mathematics and Science National Assessments (1995) at Key Stages 1, 2 and 3

Table 1.1a Reading and English

Level	KS1 Boys (%)	Reading Girls (%)	KS2 Boys (%)	English Girls (%)	KS3 Boys (%)	English Girls (%)
10					0	0
9					0	0
8					0	1
7					2	4
6			0	0	12	21
5			5	10	31	38
4	0	0	37	46	32	24
3	28	39	43	35	13	6
2	45	44	9	4	3	1
1	24	16	2	1	1	0
Other	3	1	4	4	6	5

Table 1.1b Mathematics

Level	KS1 Boys (%)	KS1 Girls (%)	KS2 Boys (%)	KS2 Girls (%)	KS3 Boys (%)	KS3 Girls (%)
10					0	0
9					0	0
8					2	1
7					9	9
6			0	0	23	23
5			13	12	23	25
4	0	0	31	33	21	21
3	21	18	36	37	12	11
2	56	63	7	6	2	2
1	19	17	2	1	0	0
Other	4	2	10	9	8	8

Table 1.1c

Science

Level	KS1 Boys (%)	KS1 Girls (%)	KS2 Boys (%)	KS2 Girls (%)	KS3 Boys (%)	KS3 Girls (%)
10					0	0
9					0	0
8					0	0
7					8	6
6			0	0	19	17
5			24	20	30	31
4	0	0	47	48	23	26
3	15	14	17	20	10	11
2	68	72	4	4	2	2
1	15	14	0	0	0	0
Other	2	0	8	8	8	7

- Boys and girls have recently been performing at very similar levels in Key Stage tests in Mathematics.

The results in Science provide another dimension to the overall picture. Teachers at Key Stage 1 assessed the competence of seven-year-olds in pretty similar terms. Eighty-six per cent of girls were judged to have achieved the 'expected level' or above compared with 83% of boys (Figure 1.1), whilst some 14% of girls were judged to have reached level 3 compared with 15% of boys (see Table 1.1c). Male and female performance in the various sub-areas of Science (scientific investigation, life and living processes, materials and their properties and physical processes) was also assessed as broadly comparable. By Key Stage 2, however, a small gender gap was beginning to appear. Twenty-four per cent of 11-year-old boys scored at level 5 or above compared with 20% of girls. This gap continued into Key Stage 3 where 27% of 14-year-old boys achieved level 6 or above compared with 23% of girls. Again, teachers' assessments presented a similar picture.

- After making comparable starts to the learning of Science, boys have begun to pull ahead of girls by Key Stage 2.

There are three other broad lessons to be drawn from the Key Stage evidence:

- Blanket statements about girls performing better than boys or vice versa are difficult to justify; reference should always be made to a *specific aspect* of the curriculum.

- Both boys and girls are to be found in roughly equal proportions at *all* levels of performance; the commonalities are as important as the differences.

- Around one-in-five seven-year-old boys and girls get off to a poor start (i.e. they are assessed at level 1) in Reading, Mathematics or Science.

1.2 PERFORMANCE IN PUBLIC EXAMINATIONS

Prior to the introduction of national testing the statistic routinely available for monitoring the performance of the educational system was the proportion of pupils obtaining five or more grades A*–C in public examinations at 16-plus. The proportions getting over this traditionally 'high hurdle' have been rising in recent years.

Recent evidence is presented in Figure 1.2 along with summary statistics for other lower hurdles. In 1995, some 48% of girls secured five or more A*–C passes in the GCSE examination compared with only 39% of boys. There were also differences, albeit smaller ones, at the lower hurdles. Nine per cent of boys and 7% of girls, for example, secured no graded passes whatsoever.

Figure 1.2

Pupils' overall performance at GCSE in 1995

% of pupils

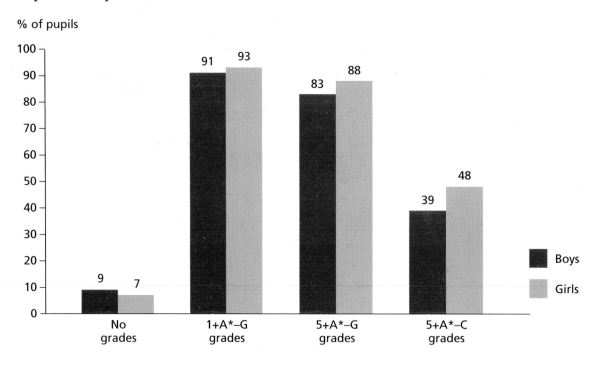

Table 1.2a demonstrates that girls sustained their superior performance in English at Key Stages 1, 2 and 3 through to GCSE. In 1995, 14% of girls secured A*/A grades compared with 8% of boys. Bearing in mind that the number of male and female candidates was roughly the same, some 66% of girls secured an A* to C grade compared with only 49% of boys.

The picture was more balanced in Mathematics. In 1995 two per cent more boys than girls obtained A*/A grades. However, taking A* to C grades overall the differences evened out; 45% of boys and 44% of girls reached this level (see Table 1.2a).

The current position in Science is much more difficult to establish. In Combined Science, by far the most popular of the Science curricula, the number of male and female entries in 1995 was roughly comparable as were the grades they achieved. Forty-seven per cent of boys and 48% of girls secured A*–C grades in 1995 (see Table 1.2b). Only a small minority of candidates were entered for one (or more) of the three separate sciences (Biology, Chemistry and Physics). The proportions of boys and girls gaining A*–C grades in Chemistry and Physics were very similar at well over 80%. However, it should be noted that rather more boys were entered for these two subjects than girls. In Biology, where the entries were more closely matched, boys did a little better than girls; on the other hand, in the Other Sciences area girls did a little better than boys (see Table 1.2b). Interpretation of the evidence on performance in Science at GCSE is complicated by these factors, but when the figures are combined across the science subjects, the boys seem to have the edge.

Table 1.2a

Performance at GCSE in English and Mathematics in 1995

Grade of Award	English		Mathematics	
	Boys (%)	Girls (%)	Boys (%)	Girls (%)
A/A*	7.7	14.2	9.5	7.4
B	15.8	23.1	13.3	13.3
C	25.3	28.4	22.7	23.6
D	23.6	20.0	16.5	17.7
E	14.6	9.0	15.9	16.4
F	9.0	4.0	12.8	12.8
G	3.2	1.1	6.8	6.5
U	0.8	0.5	2.5	2.3

Table 1.2b

Performance at GCSE in Science in 1995

| | % of A*–C Grades | | No. of Entries | |
	Boys (%)	Girls (%)	Boys (000)	Girls (000)
Combined Science	47	48	497	500
Biology	78	71	31	28
Chemistry	84	85	28	16
Physics	85	86	28	15
Other Sciences	51	65	8	6

- By 1995, girls were outperforming boys at GCSE in terms of the proportions obtaining five or more higher grade passes.

This overall conclusion needs to be qualified to some extent, however, by the differences in the separate 'core' subjects.

- Girls outperformed boys by some considerable distance in English; in Science boys maintained a small advantage; whilst in Mathematics performance was basically similar.

Some Striking Changes?

Some of the findings reported in the previous section are long-standing. The pioneering study *From Birth to Seven*, which followed up a national cohort of children born in 1958, showed that girls got off to a better start in reading (Davie *et al*, 1972). The position in arithmetic was reversed; boys had a small advantage in terms of 'problem arithmetic' and number work but their lead was not as great as that of girls in reading. Other evidence suggests, however, that there have been considerable changes in performance over the last decade. These mainly relate to secondary schooling where statistical records have been more extensive. There may have been comparable changes at the primary stages as well but, unfortunately, there is insufficient evidence to tell.

In recent years the superior performance of girls in public examinations taken at 16-plus is evident. Figure 1.3 reworks the DfEE's statistics over the last two decades to ensure that the 'gap' between males and girls, in terms of the proportions getting five or more A*–C passes, is expressed in a common metric.

Figure 1.3

Changing levels of performance at GCE/CSE or GCSE (1975–1995): number of boys per 100 girls securing 5+ A*–C grades

No. of Boys per 100 Girls

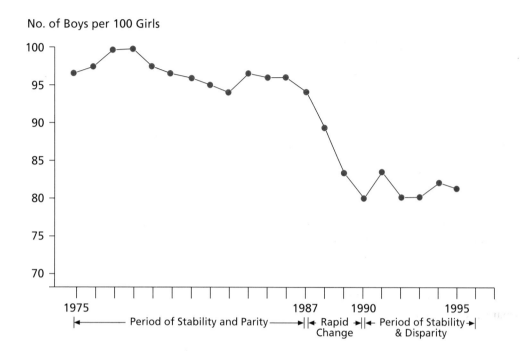

Three distinct stages can be identified. During the first of these (1975-1987) the proportions of boys and girls getting over the five or more A*–C passes hurdle was roughly comparable. For every 100 girls reaching this level of achievement there were between 94 and 100 boys, depending upon which year is selected. By the third period (1990–1995), this proportion had fallen to between 80 and 83 boys for every 100 girls. Although girls' advantage may have been thought to be a very recent phenomenon, this position appears to have been true for some six years.

Figure 1.3 shows that the changes occurred very rapidly indeed. In 1987 some 94 boys were getting over the hurdle for every 100 girls; in 1988 the figure was 89; in 1989 it was 83; and in 1990 it was 80. The changes were confined to this higher hurdle; the proportions of boys relative to girls securing the lower levels of performance reported in Figure 1.2 earlier have remained fairly constant since the mid-seventies.[3]

- The gender gap in performance in relation to the five or more A*–C passes hurdle emerged at the end of the 1980s; within four years the position had changed from one of rough equality between the sexes to clear disparity.

Between 1987 and 1990 considerable changes were introduced into the educational system in the form of the GCSE examination and latterly in terms of the National Curriculum. This was the first time that there had been a common examination for all pupils in which all levels of performance were rewarded on a common scale. At almost the same time the initial frameworks for the National Curriculum began to be introduced. Pupils were required to study quite a sizeable core of subjects until a relatively late stage in their school careers. The two developments seem to have combined to produce a situation in which more pupils were entered for more examinations because they had: (a) already studied the subjects up to a point where awards at GCSE were a reasonable prospect; and (b) were not penalised for 'inappropriate' entries since all levels of performance were rewarded on a common scale.

Another part of the explanation for these changes is a consequence of the changing patterns of subject entry which have been occurring over the past decade. A recent analysis of English and Welsh examination data (between 1984–1994) undertaken for the EOC provides important evidence on this topic (Arnot, David and Weiner, 1996). This study reported that there had been a considerable increase over this period in GCSE entries across the board with the gender entry gap 'closing substantially' in most subjects. Furthermore, whilst one could still talk of subjects which were 'dominated' by boys or girls, the general trend has been for the gender entry gaps to decrease in *most* subjects over the period from the mid-eighties to the mid-nineties.

Table 1.3 provides a more detailed picture of these changes over the last ten years. In only a small number of subjects was there a 'balanced entry', meaning that the proportions of boys and girls entering them were roughly equal; English and Mathematics were included in this group. In some other subjects, however, one sex or the other still predominates. In 1994 Physics, Design and Technology and Economics, for example, were still male provinces; furthermore, whilst the gender entry gap in favour of boys was narrowing in Physics and Design and Technology, it was actually increasing in Economics. The widening gap over the last decade in Chemistry and Computer Studies also needs to be noted; both these subjects are becoming more 'male-dominated' than in the past.

By contrast, Home Economics, Social Studies and Vocational Studies remain female provinces. Furthermore, whilst the gender entry gap in favour of girls has narrowed in Home Economics (a subject which has recently been incorporated into Technology),[4] it has increased in the other two subjects. The gender entry gaps in other subjects were less striking.

Table 1.3

Changes in the gender gap in entry to different subjects at GCSE (1984–1994)

Size of Gap in 1994	Boys Predominate	Balanced Entry	Girls Predominate	Trend in Gap Over Last Decade
Large (30%+)	Physics			Decreasing
	CDT			Decreasing
	Economics			Increasing
			Home Economics	Decreasing
			Social Studies	Increasing
			Vocational Studies	Increasing
Sizeable (15–30%)	Chemistry			Increasing
	Computer Studies			Increasing
Small (5–15%)	Technology			Decreasing
	Geography			Decreasing
			Mod. Foreign Languages	Decreasing
			English Lit.	Decreasing
No Gap (less than 5% either way)	Science			Decreasing
			Biology	Decreasing
		English		No change
		Mathematics		No change
		History		No change
		Art & Design		No change

- The size and nature of the gender gap in GCSE entries differs from subject to subject. Some subjects remain 'male-dominated' whilst others remain 'female-dominated'. Only in a minority of subjects (including English and Mathematics) has the gap been largely eliminated.

Higher levels of entry have, in turn, become translated into changed patterns of performance. It is a complex business to compare the performance levels of the two sexes in different subjects since one can never be sure, in a situation of gender-related choices where only English and Mathematics are likely to be taken by the vast majority of students, that the profiles of candidates in particular subjects are strictly comparable. Nonetheless, two features of the subject-by-subject statistics stand out from the analysis (Arnot *et al*, 1996):

- Boys secured only modest improvements over the decade in their performance at GCSE (A*–C grades) in various subjects in comparison with girls.

- Girls achieved sizeable improvements in their performance at GCSE (A*–C grades) in Science and Mathematics.[5]

1.3 DEVELOPMENTS IN THE POST-COMPULSORY SECTOR

The changes which occurred in relation to GCSE have not been matched to anything like the same extent at A-level even though there have been striking changes in levels of participation in A-level study. Here some gender disparities have persisted while others have grown wider.

Comparisons of performance across all public examinations at the post-compulsory stage are difficult to undertake because there is no common system of examining. A-levels are not studied by a majority of the young people in any particular age-group. Furthermore, even at A-level, comparisons are complicated by several factors. The most important of these is that differing proportions of boys and girls proceed to A-level study. In 1995 about one-third of boys did so compared with about two-fifths of girls. Other considerations include the fact that students have the freedom to choose the number of subjects they will study as well as the combinations; that they choose from a wide range of subjects which sometimes employ different grading procedures; and that they opt for different subjects in differing proportions. Researchers have made some attempts to take these concerns into account but have not, as yet, fully resolved them. Consequently comparisons of performance at A-level need to be treated cautiously.

The most common yardstick in use (and the one employed in the annual performance tables) is the total points score which is built up from the grades students achieve in different A/AS-level subjects. Table 1.4 below shows the distribution of scores across the full range of students studying two or more such subjects. It would appear that slightly more male students secured the highest numbers of points: 10% of boys, for example, achieved 30 or more points compared with 7% of girls. However, this male advantage has become very slight in recent years. Using another statistic in common use (the average number of points per pupil), there was really no difference at all. In 1995, boys averaged 14.5 points and girls 14.4 points (see Table 1.4).

Table 1.4
Overall performance at A-level in 1995

Total Points Score at GCE A/AS-level	Male (%)	Female (%)	All (%)
35+	4	2	3
30-34	6	5	6
25-29	9	10	9
20-24	16	18	17
15-19	13	14	14
10-14	21	22	21
5-9	15	14	14
0-4	16	15	16
Average Points Score per student	14.5	14.4	14.4
Standard Deviation	10.2	9.4	9.8

Note: the table is confined to 17+-year-old students who entered for two or more GCE A/AS-levels.

> • The virtual elimination of the gap in overall performance in A/AS-level subjects in favour of boys is a recent phenomenon which has only become evident in the last two or three years.[6]

Whilst overall performance levels appear to have evened out, there were still considerable disparities between the two sexes in terms of entries. In 'female-dominated' subjects, such as English and Modern Foreign Languages, there is still a large entry gap in favour of girls. However, it has been decreasing over the last decade (see Table 1.5); more male students have been taking these subjects.

In contrast, in 'male-dominated' subjects such as Physics, Mathematics, Computer Studies, Economics and Technology, there has still been a large gap in entries. There has been no narrowing of the entry gap in Mathematics and Computer Studies over the last decade whilst in Physics, Technology and Economics, male dominance in terms of entry has actually increased over time.

Most striking of all is the demonstration in the EOC's study that there were no major A-level subjects in the mid-nineties which were entered by equal proportions of male and female students other than History. Furthermore, there were no other subjects where one could even begin to describe the entry gap as small (see Table 1.5).

The implications of such gender-stereotyped choices of subjects post-16 are considerable, especially when female students' access to further training in scientific and technological areas is considered. A fairly recent analysis (Cheng *et al*, 1995) has shown that some 56% of male students studying for two or more A-levels were taking some science- or maths-based course compared with only 40% of female students. Forty-five per cent of boys were studying Mathematics compared with 22% of girls; and 45% of boys were also studying a physical science compared with 20% of girls. Only in the biological life sciences did female students predominate; 26% of girls were studying a subject in this area compared with 17% of boys.

Table 1.5

Changes in gender gap in entry to different subjects at A-level (1984–1994)

Size of Gap in 1994	Boys Predominate	Balanced Entry	Girls Predominate	Trend in Gap Over Last Decade
Large (30%+)	Physics			Increasing
	Mathematics			No change
	Computer Studies			No change
	Technology			Increasing
	Economics			Increasing
	CDT			Increasing
			English	Decreasing
			Mod. Foreign Languages	Decreasing
Sizeable (15–30%)	Chemistry			No change
	Geography			No change
			Biology	Decreasing
			Social Studies	Increasing
			Art & Design	Decreasing
Small (5–15%)	none		none	
No Gap (less than 5% either way)			History	Decreasing

- Gender-related patterns of entry have persisted in the majority of A-level subjects over much of the past decade; the number of subjects in which a (fairly) balanced entry has emerged over time has been very modest.

Improved levels of performance amongst 16-year-old female students have contributed to increases in those staying on in education. Table 1.6a shows that the proportions of male and female students undertaking either full- or part-time courses post-16 over the last decade jumped from just below two-thirds of the age-group to around four-fifths. Increases in the tendency to stay on at 16 have, in turn, become translated into higher participation rates post-18 where the numbers on full-time courses have more than doubled. Again, the improvement in the position of young women on such courses has been rather greater than that of the young men with the result that the proportions engaged in both full- and part-time courses at this stage have become roughly equal (see Table 1.6b).

Table 1.6a

Changing patterns of post-16 participation (1985–1995)

		1985 (%)	1992 (%)	1995 (%)
Full-time courses	Males	43	63	69
	Females	51	71	75
Part-time courses	Males	20	11	9
	Females	16	8	7
All courses	Males	63	74	77
	Females	66	79	81

Table 1.6b

Changing patterns of post-18 participation (1985–1995)

		1985 (%)	1992 (%)	1995 (%)
Full-time courses	Males	17	28	38
	Females	16	29	39
Part-time courses	Males	17	17	11
	Females	10	9	8
All courses	Males	34	45	49
	Females	26	38	47

Whilst there has been a general trend for both sexes to stay on post-16, young women have not only increased their enrolment on A/AS-level courses over the last decade but increased it relative to young men. In 1985 around one-in-five young men and women in the age cohort were studying for A/AS-levels; by 1995 around two-fifths (39%) of young women were taking this route compared with one-third (33%) of the young men.[7]

Changes in other courses are more difficult to establish because of the recent introduction of national vocational qualifications (GNVQs) and the absence of a comparable framework a decade previously. In general the recent patterns of male and female enrolment appear to be fairly similar. Roughly equal proportions have been studying for Advanced GNVQs, NVQs at Level 3 and Intermediate and Foundation GNVQs but the percentages in national terms within each of these three broad areas are very small when compared with enrolments at A-level. Enrolments on Intermediate & Foundation GNVQs and NVQ Levels 1 and 2 have been more substantial but there are no obvious disparities between the sexes.[8] About one-in-five young men have been taking such courses and a very similar proportion of young women (see DfEE, 1995, Table 1.3).

On the other hand, the subjects male and female students have chosen for vocational preparation have differed quite markedly. Some 36% of male students were studying for at least one Mathematics or Science-based subject compared with only 16% of female students (Cheng *et al*, 1995). Twenty-five per cent of young men had chosen at least one subject from the engineering, technology and architecture area compared with only 2% of young women; and 14% of young men were doing something in the mathematics/computing area compared with only 6% of young women. There again, no young men were studying a medical or life science subject for a vocational qualification compared with some 8% of young women. Looking beyond the science/mathematics area more young women were enrolled in business and social studies subjects (75% of female students compared with 56% of male students).

- Gender-stereotyping in the mid-nineties among the 16–19 age-group in terms of the subjects studied for vocational qualifications is just as strong as at A-level.

The general increase in the enrolments of both sexes in higher education has been the most notable phenomenon of the last decade – participation rates have more than doubled (DfEE, 1995). In 1985 around 8% of both sexes in the age-cohort were engaged in some form of higher education (at degree or sub-degree level); by 1995 these figures had risen to some 19% of young men and some 20% of young women.

- Gender differences in access to higher education appear not to have changed much in the last decade; both sexes have more than doubled their levels of participation.

1.4 ACADEMIC PROGRESS

In this section the evidence about whether one sex makes more rapid academic progress during the course of their school career is considered. We tackled this question in two related ways. First, we conducted a straw poll of leading researchers who have tracked pupils' educational progress between Key Stages 1 and 2 or between Key Stages 2 and 4. We asked them whether they routinely took gender into account in their analyses and, if so, why. They all reported that they did so. By far the most important predictor, however, of how well a pupil would perform at some later date (say, Key Stage 2) was how well they had already performed at some earlier time-point (say, Key Stage 1).[9]

Other research evidence supports the assessments of what makes a difference to pupils' progress between the various time-points and the relative importance of gender in relation to other variables. In the *School Matters* study, for example, girls made slightly greater progress between the ages of 7-plus and 10-plus in inner London primary schools (Mortimore *et al*, 1988). Nearly all the studies that have tracked pupils between the ages of 11 and 16 have reached similar conclusions (see Gray and Wilcox, 1995 and Sammons, 1996 for some estimates). Furthermore, the only recent study which followed up pupils from the age of seven to the age of 16 reports that gender made some difference; girls progressed a little faster (Sammons *et al*, 1995).

Increasingly large numbers of schools are undertaking some form of value-added analysis of their pupils' performances. These research findings suggest that when groups of boys and girls of 'similar performance' at, say, age 11 (measured, perhaps, in terms of reading or mathematics tests or verbal or non-verbal reasoning assessments) are compared at some later stage (say GCSE), one would predict that the girls would be slightly ahead.

- Girls have made somewhat greater academic progress between the ages of seven and 16 than boys.

Levels of academic progress have been reversed, however, at A-level. A recent DfEE analysis compared students with the same levels of performance at GCSE (DfEE, 1996d). Amongst the less well-qualified at GCSE, the differences between male and female students in terms of A-level points were small or non-existent (see Figure 1.4); however, amongst candidates with higher average GCSE scores differences began to emerge. Male students who did well at GCSE made greater progress than female students to the extent of about half a grade per subject entered.

Figure 1.4:

Performance at A-level (1995) by prior performance at GCSE

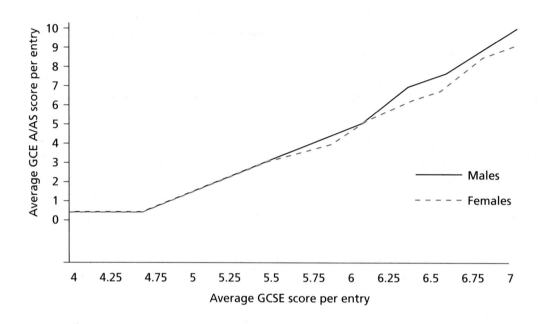

- Boys made somewhat greater academic progress between GCSE and A-level than girls.

When the evidence on the gaps in performance between male and female students is considered along with evidence on the academic progress they make, it becomes clear that a modest part of these differences *may* be attributable to differences in the school experiences of the two groups. This is an issue which we shall explore in greater depth in Chapter 4.

1.5 INTERNATIONAL COMPARISONS

There have been a number of international studies of pupil achievement over the last two decades which merit attention, although they are frequently difficult to interpret.[10] The *Worlds Apart?* review for OFSTED has, for example, already established that pupils in England have not fared particularly well. In international comparisons over the last decade, the country has usually found itself somewhere in the middle of the pack and, on occasion, just a little behind it (Reynolds and Farrell, 1996), although the position varies somewhat according to the age ranges, subjects, the nature of the skills and tasks being compared, and the countries being compared in any one study.

The evidence from national assessment programmes has recently been helpfully summarised by Johnson (1996). Like our own national testing, nearly all the major studies she considered have covered the areas of language, mathematics and science although they have not always included the same sub-topics under these headings; they have also differed in the ways in which these subjects have been assessed. Nevertheless, they report findings which are strikingly similar to those described in Section 1.1.

In the United States, Australia, Scotland and Holland, for example, girls seem to have got off to a better start in terms of learning to read and write. Studies from these countries, and Canada as well, confirm that girls sustained this advantage amongst the older age-groups.[11]

The picture with respect to Mathematics is a little more complicated and depends, in part, on which particular aspect of performance is being assessed. Revisiting Johnson's summary table of the girl/boy differences, it is clear that there has been a tendency for boys to do better than girls as they progress through school. Overall, however, the differences have been modest until the late teens and compensated, to some extent, by different patterns in different sub-areas of Mathematics.[12]

Clearer patterns of gender-related differences emerge from the international comparisons of performance in Science. Boys are usually reported to be doing better than girls (see Johnson, 1996, Table 1.4). The largest differences are found in relation to aspects of physical science; boys' advantage in this area has emerged as early as the primary stages and tended to get larger as they progress through school. The boys' advantage has usually been smaller in biology and chemistry but, nonetheless, evident. Hardly any of the studies have shown girls doing consistently better within particular sub-areas.

Many of the studies Johnson reviewed are now dated and even the most recent was several years old.[13] It is against this background that the evidence from the Third International Mathematics and Science Study (TIMSS) is interesting (Keys et al, 1996). This survey was conducted as recently as 1995 and covered a national sample of English pupils in years 8 and 9.

Pupils' results in England are reported within the context of 40 other countries. In terms of Mathematics, for example, they were just a little below the international average. In Science, however, they did rather better, outperforming some two-thirds of the other countries.

The differences between boys and girls in England in terms of Mathematics were negligible amongst the year 9 group. Year 9 boys were a little ahead in all areas of Science, although only in the areas dubbed Physics and Chemistry were the differences really noticeable and hardly any of these were statistically significant.

- Pupils in England do not show up particularly well in international comparisons. Gender-related patterns of performance are not dissimilar from those in comparable societies. Girls seem to do better in Language across the world. The position in Mathematics up to the age of 16 seems to be more evenly matched. In Science, however, there are signs that girls have begun to fall behind as early as the age of 11; again this is a world-wide phenomenon.

Sources of Statistical Data Used in Figures and Tables

Figure 1.1 and Tables 1.1a, 1.1b and 1.1c: based on three reports from DfEE (1996a,b,c) *Results of the 1995 National Curriculum Assessments of 7 year olds/11 year olds/ 14 year olds in England;* **Figure 1.2:** table provided by the DfEE Analytical Services Branch, 'The GCSE/O/CSE Achievements of Pupils in Schools in England 1974/75 to 1994/95'; **Tables 1.2a and 1.2b:** The Joint Council for the General Certificate of Secondary Education (1995) *Inter-Group Statistics Summer 1995: Volume 1 - Grades Analysed by Gender,* Guildford: Southern Examining Group; **Figure 1.3:** based on table provided by the DfEE Analytical Services Branch, 'The GCSE/O/CSE Achievements of Pupils in Schools in England 1974/75 to 1994/95; **Table 1.3:** based on evidence collated in M. Arnot, M. David and G. Weiner (1996) *Educational Reforms and Gender Equality in Schools,* Manchester: Equal Opportunities Commission, Appendix B, Tables B.1 and B.2; **Table 1.4** DfEE (1996) *GCSE and GCE A/AS Level Performance of Candidates Attempting Two or More GCE A/AS Levels in 1994/95,* Statistical Bulletin 2/96, Tables 11 and 12 and evidence from Dr Sally Thomas of the London University Institute of Education; **Table 1.5:** see Table 1.3; **Tables 1.6a and 1.6b:** DfEE (1995) *Participation in Education and Training by 16-18 Year Olds in England: 1984/85 to 1994/95,* London: Department for Education and Employment, Table 1.2 and Table 1.3; **Figure 1.4:** DfEE (1996d) *GCSE and GCE A/AS Level Performance of Candidates Attempting Two or More GCE A/AS Levels in 1994/95,* Statistical Bulletin, 2/96, Chart C.

---

[1] See annexes to three separate reports from the DfEE (1996). *Results from the 1995 National Curriculum Assessments of Seven Year Olds/Eleven Year Olds/Fourteen Year Olds in England,* London: Department for Education and Employment.

[2] See annexes to the three reports referred to in footnote 1.

[3] See table provided by the DfEE Analytical Services Branch entitled 'The GCSE/O/CSE Achievements of Pupils in Schools in England 1974/75 to 1994/5' which forms the basis of Figure 1.2. In making comparisons over such lengthy periods of time, one needs to bear in mind a couple of caveats. In particular, the examination system has changed. Until 1988 pupils were entered for O-levels and CSEs with the assumption that a grade 1 at CSE was equivalent to a grade C at O-level. Since 1988 pupils have been entered for the GCSE, a common examination for all. The surveys on which Figure 1.3 is based have also been modified at various stages. Fortunately, neither of these considerations is likely to have biased the evidence unduly in favour of one sex or the other.

[4] CDT and aspects of Home Economics have now become part of Design and Technology within Technology in the National Curriculum.

[5] For further details see Chapter 4 and Appendix B in Arnot, David and Weiner, 1996.

[6] See evidence used as sources for Table 1.4.

[7] See sources for Tables 1.6a and 1.6b.

[8] See sources for Tables 1.6a and 1.6b.

[9] Entitlement to free school meals (a measure of poverty) was also frequently referred to. Most researchers felt that three factors (prior attainment followed by gender and free school meals) were well worth building routinely into their analyses.

[10] The major ones have been conducted by the International Association for the Evaluation of Educational Achievement (the IEA) and Educational Testing Services in the USA. Between them they haveconducted over a dozen studies comparing performance across countries.

[11] See Johnson (1996), Table 1.2 for fuller details.

[12] See Johnson (1996), Table 1.3.

[13] See Brown (1996) for fuller discussion of the strengths and weaknesses of the first two Mathematics and Science surveys. Some of these weaknesses have been overcome in TIMMS.

PART 2

SCHOOL ORGANISATION AND PROCESSES

2 CURRICULUM, TEACHING AND LEARNING

In this chapter we ask whether aspects of the curriculum, teaching and learning contribute to gendered patterns in outcomes. We concentrate on research that has been reported since 1988, the first year when 16-year-olds took the GCSE.

2.1 TEACHING AND CLASSROOM PROCESSES

In 1988 Kelly published a meta-analysis[1] of 81 studies that yielded some quantifiable data on teacher–pupil interactions with respect to gender. She concluded: 'It is now beyond dispute that girls receive less of the teacher's attention in class, and that this is true across a wide range of different conditions' (p.20). However, her review did not unearth studies that linked teacher–pupil interaction with performance, suggesting that it was still a matter of supposition that more teacher attention produces better outcomes.

A more recent review of gender dimensions of teacher–pupil and pupil–pupil interaction in primary and secondary classrooms has been carried out by Howe (1997). Her review is organised in relation to the range of teaching arrangements that characterise most of what goes on in classrooms from nursery to sixth forms including whole-class teaching and group work. Across all these teaching contexts a number of key points emerge:

- Contributions from boys are prominent both physically and verbally during classroom interaction.

- Girls request help from others to a greater extent than boys.

- Boys have more experience than girls of having their contributions evaluated during classroom interaction, both by teachers and peers, and both negatively and positively.

- These patterns are established at a very early age in pre-school, nursery and infant school classrooms.

Gender differences in classroom *processes* are therefore present but their significance for educational *performance* is not self-evident. There is little research that directly links classroom interaction with academic outcomes. In view of the current interest in the effectiveness of different teaching methods and different forms of classroom organisation, this could be a fruitful area for future research.

Some recent research suggests that patterns of classroom interaction are of *indirect* relevance through their impact upon attitudes and learning strategy. For example, Crump (1990) found that although male behaviours and attitudes 'robbed' girls of teacher time in many classrooms, this did not necessarily advantage boys. A convergence between the cultural perspectives of teachers and girls allowed them to maintain confidence in their academic competence, which was recognised by themselves, their teachers and by most male pupils. There is also some evidence that girls adopt effective 'compensatory strategies', such as approaching teachers individually, to ensure that their questions are answered and their needs are met. In other words, whilst boys develop a more public learning strategy, girls have a more private strategy. One aspect of such a private strategy might be girls' more committed and conscientious approach to homework.[3]

> • Patterns of classroom interaction may have fewer implications for pupils' performance than for the development of attitudes and strategies.

2.2 CURRICULUM CONTENT AND THE GENDER IMAGES OF SUBJECTS

Much research during the 1970s and 1980s investigated the extent to which aspects of the curriculum, and subjects in particular, had been 'gendered' and whether this could be attributed to the kind of learning demanded, the messages in curriculum texts, or staffing patterns in schools. There is now a vast amount of research in this area, especially in relation to the different school subjects. There is insufficient space here to attempt a comprehensive review, so we have simply selected research that illuminates issues with relevance across the curriculum.

Changes in Definitions of Subject Knowledge and Pupils' Responses to Learning Demands

The introduction of the GCSE, the National Curriculum, NVQs and GNVQs has contributed to changes in the way different kinds of knowledge are valued. In many curricular areas there has been a move away from an almost exclusive emphasis on learning in terms of propositional knowledge (knowledge of facts) towards more emphasis on process knowledge (knowledge of application in different contexts). Definitions of competence, which are central to new forms of vocational education, incorporate both aspects, although a debate still rages about the appropriate balance in academic curricula. Some researchers suggest that these shifts in the learning demands made of pupils may also have contributed to recent shifts in the relative performance of male and female pupils.

In Australia there has been a definite move away from memorising facts, which can be tested in short-answer exercises, towards extended tasks that require pupils to apply their learning. They are asked to produce written portfolios, extended prose and research projects. This kind of learning usually requires high levels of sustained attention. A large study (Hill *et al*, 1993) of 14,000 students (from reception to age 17) in 90 Australian schools found that teachers rated girls as significantly more attentive in class and this was positively correlated with higher levels of achievement and rates of progress than boys. Attentiveness/inattentiveness, therefore, was thought to be the most consistent and salient factor in explaining boys' and girls' relative performance. The researchers conclude that changes in what pupils are expected to learn has placed a greater premium on attentiveness which has, in turn, contributed to substantial gender differences in performance.

A much smaller English study (Boaler, 1997) supports the general view that boys and girls differ in their attitudes to learning and in their preferences for different ways of 'knowing'. Moreover, these differences appear to influence outcomes. Using tests, observations and interviews, Boaler studied a year group of pupils in each of two schools over a three-year period as they moved from year 9 to year 11. The schools were located in similar areas and the pupils had similar scores on cognitive abilities tests at the beginning of year 9. However, the schools had very different approaches to the teaching of mathematics. In one, the mathematics department adopted a traditional, content-led, textbook-based approach; in the other, the approach was more open and project-based with an emphasis on process.

Boaler found that there were significant differences in the attainment of boys and girls at the two schools. Boys and girls had similar achievements in terms of A to C grades in GCSE mathematics at the school with the project-based approach, but the girls significantly underachieved at the school with the traditional approach. Furthermore, this underachievement was most acute in the top set.

Interviews with pupils indicated that girls achieved less in the traditional teaching environment because they became disaffected by pace, pressure, competitiveness and closed approaches. They desired the time and space to think and discuss, so that they could achieve understanding. Boys also preferred open, discussion-based work but they were more prepared than girls to adapt to an approach they disliked. This gave boys an advantage in tests and exercises involving speed, rules and correct answers.

We do want to emphasise that this was a study of only two schools and clearly it would be dangerous to make firm generalisations to apply to other schools. Although this study attributes differences in performance between pupils to teaching methods and learning styles, there may be other factors that play an equally important part. However, Boaler's hypothesis is worthy of further testing.

Boaler claims that her observations are consistent with those of Gilligan and others[4] who have suggested that, as a consequence of the specific socialisation practices in the development of boys and girls, different 'ways of knowing' emerge. 'Separate knowing' is based on the use of impersonal procedures to establish truths and is favoured by men, whereas 'connected knowing', favoured by women, builds on personal experience and involves consideration and integration of a wide range of understandings that have a bearing on a situation or problem.[5]

- There is evidence that girls are more attentive in class and more willing to learn. They do better than boys on sustained tasks that are open-ended, process-based, related to realistic situations, and that require pupils to think for themselves.

- Boys show greater adaptability to more traditional approaches to learning which require memorising abstract, unambiguous facts and rules that have to be acquired quickly. They also appear to be more willing to sacrifice deep understanding, which requires sustained effort, for correct answers achieved at speed.

In earlier but important work on mathematics teaching, Walkerdine (1989) makes similar points about masculine and feminine ways of knowing. Her studies remind us that the way subject knowledge is defined is not solely the responsibility of curriculum and syllabus designers. She illustrated how the nature of what counts as performance is also actively influenced by teachers in classrooms. Teachers rarely offered girls opportunities to become 'brilliant' mathematicians. Rationality, imagination and elegance of solution were competences associated with male styles of work; girls were viewed as naturally unable to achieve such high levels of intellect.

English, on the other hand, is seen as a 'feminine' subject from an early age. This may be because boys are not yet mature enough when reading is taught and girls learn faster, and also because it is women who usually teach children to read or are seen to read books or to write in the home.[6] Such polarisation is reaffirmed as children go through school. Martino (1994), studying 16- and 17-year-olds in Australia, found clear differences in the way boys and girls perceived English and concluded that 'boys tend to undervalue English as a feminised learning practice'. The main reasons the boys gave for regarding English as more suited to girls was because it was a sedentary activity, it dealt with personal response to text and was irrelevant to the 'real' world.

A large part of the curriculum in English focuses on reading and writing fictional stories. Millard (1996) found that boys (and teachers) are often unaware that their out-of-school reading also counts as literacy. Meanwhile White (1986) and Alloway and Gilbert (1997) have suggested that boys' preferences for non-fiction may actually be more enabling than disabling, sometimes contributing more to a successful career than the school-related activities in which girls do well.

- Boys perceive the literacy experience as female because, from an early age, reading and writing are associated with feminine forms of expression, especially the exploration of personal experience and feelings in stories and poetry. The value of reading and writing non-fiction, and combining physical and verbal activity in the study and acting of plays, may be insufficiently acknowledged and developed in the curriculum. This may disadvantage boys and possibly girls.

Such studies are illustrative of the kind of attention that has been paid to gender issues in relation to 'core' subjects such as English and mathematics. However, studies of non-core subjects also raise questions about the nature and pedagogy of subjects and whether these exhibit gender bias in ways that affect performance.

A study conducted in five London schools (Paechter and Head, 1996) indicates that the new subject, Design and Technology, which incorporates the older subjects of Craft, Design and Technology and Home Economics, has redefined the nature of the subject domain. A new emphasis on design and evaluation has introduced more theoretical work that requires pupils to draw on their knowledge of science and technology and to produce written reports. This more academic definition of subject knowledge has raised the status of the subject and increased its perceived relevance to industrial work, but also reduced the emphasis on practical skills and skills for daily living. These changes in definitions of subject knowledge have done little to create greater gender-neutrality. The more academic orientation of the curriculum, the closer links with science and technology, the heavy weighting towards work with resistant materials (wood, metal and plastics), and the playing down of human purposes and values, are all described as evidence of an increased 'masculinisation' of the subject.

Paechter and Head also make some comparisons with PE and conclude that similar masculinisation is occurring in this subject for similar reasons. Comparable observations about the changing nature of music education are to be found in a study which investigated how pupils reacted to the introduction of music technology (computers) (Comber, Hargreaves and Colley, 1993).

Gender-stereotyped Imagery in Curriculum Materials

In the 1980s the scrutiny of school texts for gender bias was a popular activity among feminists who were concerned about the images of women portrayed in texts and their possible impact on the aspirations of girls. Most of these analyses concluded that women were largely 'invisible', portrayed in domestic contexts or in low status and marginal roles. The suggestion was that such gender images shaped pupils' attitudes to schooling in general, and their attitudes to subjects in particular, thereby influencing later choice patterns.

This strand of research has continued to be pursued in recent years but on a reduced scale. One possible reason is that the research on gender-stereotyping in curriculum materials was widely disseminated and that educational writers and publishers are now thought to be aware of the need to avoid stereotyped imagery. Another is the possibility that the focus of interest has shifted to more subtle and more hidden aspects of gender stereotyping in school subjects, such as the ways they are assessed (see Chapter 3).

Pupils' Interests, Subject Preferences and Course Choices

Recent research in pre-school and infant settings is largely consistent with earlier findings that girls' choose creative, social and domestic-related activities whilst boys choose constructive, individualistic and energetic physical activities.[7] Children appear to pursue gendered interests even when engaged in the same activity: girls might make houses with Lego, as a foil for social play, while boys might make vehicles and guns focusing on movement and balance. Such patterns are consistent across cultural and social groups and are said to contribute to the formation of gender domains.

Some evidence of slight changes in patterns of activity is, however, to be found in a study of thirty 8–9-year-olds at a middle school (Henshaw *et al*, 1992). Boys and girls were offered four tasks to test their toy preferences and attitudes towards cross-gender play. The results indicated that it was permissible for girls to choose boys' toys but not vice versa. Boys' roles were still more rigidly prescribed than girls.

Within the secondary sector much research has focused on patterns of subject choice and the reasons that might account for these. In Chapter 1 we noted a narrowing of the gender gap in patterns of entry to GCSE although there is no comparable pattern of convergence in subject choices at A-level. Indeed, post-16 gender-related patterns have persisted and in some cases increased. In searching for explanations, we need to recognise that the introduction of the National Curriculum has had the effect of *restricting* choice at GCSE, thus encouraging pupils to enter for subjects that they might avoid if they had the choice. After GCSE, these restrictions do not operate and other factors are brought to bear on choices.

A number of studies have investigated the idea that attitudes towards, and choice of, subjects are associated with perceptions of subjects on a masculine–feminine dimension. In most cases, researchers have asked pupils to rate or rank subjects in relation to this dimension, or to express subject preferences which could then be analysed by gender. Results have largely been consistent across studies and across age-cohorts.[8]

- Science, mathematics, technology, IT and PE are rated as 'masculine' by pupils and preferred by boys; English, humanities, music, PSE and RE are rated as 'feminine' and preferred by girls.

There is some evidence, nonetheless, that some subject preferences are becoming less gendered. Taylor and Mardle (1986) indicate, for example, that boys and girls both rejected the idea that mathematics and science were 'boys' subjects', although boys still showed ambivalence about crossing boundaries into traditionally female domains. And indeed, by 1991, according to Archer and Macrae (1991), mathematics, chemistry, biology and languages had become more gender neutral.

Stables and Winkeley (1996) have embarked on what is likely to be an important study to investigate the degree to which the introduction and subsequent modification of the National Curriculum has affected pupils' preferences, perceptions and the process of year 9 option choices. A preliminary analysis of 1996 interviews with pupils, drawn from the same 12 schools used in an earlier study, indicates that gender differences in subject uptake are much less marked than in 1984. However, there is still evidence of gender patterning in choices within areas such as technology, with girls favouring courses involving personal interaction. Similarly, there is some preliminary indication that parents' advice concerning options may be less gender differentiated, as are some career aspirations and leisure interests. However, boys continue to have less clear ideas about what to do after year 11 than girls and some have unrealistic expectations of career entry at 16. The researchers suggest that such naivety may prevent boys from fulfilling their educational potential.

- There is some evidence that pupils' subject preferences and choices are becoming slightly less gender-stereotyped. This change is mainly in one direction: girls are more prepared to tackle 'masculine' subjects, especially high-status subjects; boys on the other hand, continue to shun 'feminine' subjects, especially boys with stereotyped attitudes towards future occupations and roles.

A few studies have investigated subject preferences in relation to other factors. Archer and Macrae (1991), for example, found that variance in boys' subject preferences was also associated with a boring–interesting dimension, whilst girls' replies were correlated with a difficult–easy dimension. Garratt (1986) and Stables and Stables (1995) report that, although 'interest' was a major reason for girls choosing an A-level subject, 'difficulty' was mentioned as a reason for their finding courses different from expectations.

The issue of subject difficulty was also investigated by the Assessment of Performance Unit mathematics team (Joffe and Foxman, 1988). They found that one of the most marked gender differences was in pupils' perceptions of the difficulty of the subject and elements within a subject. By age 15, girls were finding mathematics significantly more difficult than boys and were enjoying it less, even when their performance was on a par. Boys tended to overrate the easiness of an item (more said it was easy than got it right) whereas girls tended to overrate the difficulty of the item (more got it right than said it was easy). This was thought to have implications for pupils' confidence and affect their choices at stages when subjects such as mathematics cease to be compulsory.

- There is evidence that girls overrate a subject's difficulty in comparison with boys.

The nature and quality of teacher–pupil relationships is another factor that is shown to be influential in the formation of pupils' subject preferences. In Younger and Warrington's (1996) study, student responses indicated that some subjects were unpopular because they were taught in a boring manner. Teaching in a formal, didactic style created a particularly strong and negative reaction from boys.

The ability of the teacher to inspire and motivate pupils also emerged as particularly important in a study of the discrepancy in attitudes and performance between boys and girls (Clark and Trafford, 1995).[9] In interviews with staff and pupils in four schools, the quality of the pupil–teacher relationship emerged as crucial for confidence-building among boys as well as girls.

Studies looking at the relationship between gender and curriculum participation rarely differentiate *within* the gender categories. Yet this is a potentially important area for research (see Lamb, 1996). More research is clearly needed on the interaction between gender and other variables, such as social class and ethnicity, in relation to subject preferences and course choices.

---

[1] Meta-analysis is a quantitative method of reviewing research which involves converting results to a common metric and conducting statistical analyses across studies to examine similarities and differences in their findings.

[2] Dart and Clarke (1988); Jones and Gerig (1994); Taber (1992).

[3] Harris *et al* (1993) and Warrington and Younger (1995).

[4] Belenky *et al* (1986); Gilligan (1982); Brown and Gilligan (1992).

5   Psychologists have long been concerned with the possibility that individuals may differ in the cognitive style through which information is apprehended and processed, and that such differences may also be related to preferences for different learning styles. In one of the earliest studies in this area, Witkin *et al* (1962) distinguished field-(or context-) dependent and independent styles and, suggested that girls were more field-dependent than boys. Subsequent research, however, has reported more mixed findings, with some researchers reporting consistent gender differences, while others have not. In part, this divergence of opinion may be attributable to differences in the research instruments used in these studies.

6   Swann (1992); Pidgeon (1993).

7   Askew and Ross (1988); Browne and Ross (1991); Delamont (1990); Hodgeon (1988).

8   Archer and Macrae (1991); Colley *et al* (1994); Stables and Stables (1995); Stables and Winkeley (1996).

9   This study focused on modern foreign languages so it is not possible to say whether this phenomenon occurred in other subjects as well.

3 THE IMPACT OF ASSESSMENT

The principal question here is whether differential achievement is actually constructed by assessment procedures. If this is so, then there is good reason to challenge the basis of the statistics given in Chapter 1 and to question whether the gender patterns represent 'real' differences. Furthermore, if there is evidence that differences in educational performance are created by the way assessments are carried out, then it may be important to review methods of assessment to achieve greater equality of opportunity. This then raises a question about whether equality in performance is a valid goal. It may be a valid goal provided that what is assessed at school level still reflects the professional discipline in a satisfactory way. For example, school science needs to be related to what is practised by scientists. However, even this relationship is not straightforward because professional disciplines are constantly changing (Burton, 1995 discusses the way in which some mathematicians are adopting more 'feminist' approaches to their discipline).

These are complex issues. A detailed and comprehensive review of research in this area is to be found in Gipps and Murphy (1994). Here we briefly consider recent research on some of the most important issues.

3.1 ENTRY PATTERNS

Two major studies (Stobart *et al*, 1992a and Elwood and Comber, 1996) have investigated entry patterns to the major academic examinations in England: GCSE and A-level. These are based mainly on data provided by the examinations boards. Unfortunately, data are not readily available from the awarding bodies for vocational qualifications so no comparable analyses have yet been carried out. The DfEE intends to create a database to which GNVQ awarding bodies will be asked to submit data on course registrations and attainments. It will then be possible to analyse patterns of course choice and performance in this area as well.

GCSE Entry Patterns

The introduction of the GCSE in 1988 provided a 'natural experiment' which allowed comparisons to be made with the O-level and CSE examinations that preceded it. Stobart *et al* (1992a) carried out analyses of entry and outcome patterns using inter-examination board statistics. They noted that girls' participation improved markedly after the introduction of the GCSE. In 1989, girls provided 51% of the total GCSE entries although they made up only 48.5% of the 16-year-old cohort. The researchers hypothesised that lower-attaining boys were not being entered while girls with similar performance in school were. They also noted imbalances in entry patterns in particular subject areas. Girls made up only 28% of the physics entry, 45% of the chemistry entry but 63% of the biology entry. They suggested that this might be evidence of a highly selective female entry for physics (which would explain why girls outperformed boys by 4% in the A*–C grades) but also of biology being regarded as a token science in their GCSE portfolio. This would explain why boys outperformed girls by 7% in the A*–C grades. As Table 1.2b in Chapter 1 indicates, the pattern in 1995 was similar. Girls still outperformed boys in physics A*–C grades, but only by a mere 1%. However, substantially larger numbers of boys (28,000) were entered than girls (15,000). In biology, boys still outperformed girls by 7% despite similar numbers of entries (31,000 to 28,000).

Differentiated entry for GCSE mathematics was also thought to contribute to differences in performance. In 1990, grades A–D could be awarded in the highest tier, C–F grades in the intermediate tier and E–G grades in the foundation tier. A higher proportion of girls were entered for the middle level – the 'safety option' – which provided the key grade C whilst avoiding the risks of being unclassified. Stobart *et al* (1992a) suggested that this was evidence of an underestimation of what female candidates could do. Since 1994, grade C has become the minimum award for the highest tier and B is maximum for the intermediate tier. In 1994, significantly more girls than boys were entered for the intermediate tier: 59% of girls as opposed to 54% of boys, a difference of 21,000 individuals.

- There is evidence that systems of tiered papers in mathematics produce different patterns of performance for boys and girls. These patterns suggest either that the performance of girls is underestimated in mathematics or that teachers enter them for the 'safe' tier to protect them from anxiety.

A-level Entries

Elwood and Comber (1996) carried out a similar investigation of gender differences in performance in A-level examinations. The results of the research indicate that important explanations for the cross-over in performance patterns post-16 relate to patterns of entry (which at A-level relate closely to the subject preferences and course choices discussed in the previous chapter). More girls now enter for A-level than boys (54% of the total entry in 1994 against 38% of the entry in 1970) but they do not leave their A-level courses better qualified. For example, in English literature, where 6% more girls gained Grade A in GCSE between 1990 and 1994, this pattern reversed dramatically and 2% more boys than girls gained Grade A at A-level during the same period.

This pattern was repeated in history and French. In physics, in which girls obtained 4% more top grades than boys in GCSE, their advantage at A-level fell to an average of 0.4% cumulative grades. Comber and Elwood (1996) explain the 8% gain that boys made in English literature by suggesting that the boys who choose this traditionally 'female' subject area are a small but very able and highly motivated group. This might also explain their success in history and French. Girls who choose the gender-stereotyped area of physics are also very able and highly motivated and it would seem reasonable to expect them to maintain their advantage. The fact that they do not suggests that other factors are also operating in their case. The more traditional approach of A-level examinations, for example, with more emphasis on terminal examinations and less varied use of assessment techniques, may benefit boys more than girls (discussed below).

- Important explanations for the cross-over in performance patterns post-16 relate to entry patterns but these need to be considered together with the possible impact of changes in mode of assessment from GCSE to A-level.

3.2 MODES OF ASSESSMENT

The research summarised below suggests that there is considerable evidence for believing that different kinds of assessment techniques produce particular patterns of results that are gender-related. Such proposals raise educational, technical, political and ethical issues to do with the validity of assessments.

Multiple-choice Tests

In large-scale surveys the gender gap changes according to the kind of instruments used. For example, cross-national studies of science, which are all based on pencil and paper multiple-choice instruments, show boys outperforming girls on most measures. Most recently, the Third International Mathematics and Science Study (TIMSS)[1] reported that, at a time when girls in England were producing science and mathematics results comparable to boys in National Curriculum tests and GCSE, boys in England were still performing considerably better than girls in TIMSS tests. The authors of the report acknowledge that the discrepancy in relation to Key Stage 3 results may be partly a function of the type of questions used because around 80% of TIMSS questions were presented in multiple-choice format.

A study of the comparative performance of 15-year-olds on multiple-choice tests and free-response tests in Irish schools (Bolger and Kellaghan, 1990) provided further confirmation of the hypothesis that boys perform significantly better than girls on multiple-choice tests. Moreover, the expectation that the gender difference would be larger for languages and smaller for mathematics, because of the superior verbal skills attributed to females, was not fulfilled.[2]

There are suggestions that multiple-choice tests favour boys because they are better suited to the 'eyes down' approach, because they can avoid having to express themselves in English, and because they have greater confidence in choosing a response as correct (even if it isn't) in contrast to girls who give greater attention to the relative rightness/wrongness of items (Stobart *et al*, 1992a) .

- There is evidence that boys perform significantly better than girls on multiple-choice tests, whatever the subject area.

Traditional 'Sudden Death' Examinations

A study of GCSE results in mathematics (Stobart *et al*, 1992b) found that boys achieved on average a small mark advantage on examination papers which offset girls' small but consistent mark advantage on coursework. Questionnaire responses from teachers in the same study indicated that they perceived girls to have difficulty with examinations because of anxieties about failure and the pressures of the occasion. However, the overall performance results indicated that these attributed anxieties did not appear to translate into erratic performances on a significant scale.

Elwood's and Comber's (1996) later research on A-level results suggests the style of A-level, which is still dominated by terminal examinations, may reward certain approaches more than others. Teachers described boys as confident, self-assured, risk taking and unperturbed by 'sudden death' exams whereas girls tended to write at length, lacked courage in discarding irrelevant material and therefore performed less well in traditional exams. Elwood and Comber conclude that the style of GCSE, with its wider range of assessment modes, may be more congenial to girls than traditional A-levels and may account for the 'cross-over' in performance post-16.

- There is some evidence that girls find timed, end-of-course examinations less congenial than do boys and this may adversely affect their performance.

Coursework Assessments

Cresswell (1990) analysed the results from the 1989 AEB GCSE examinations in English, mathematics and science (before restrictions were placed on the amount of coursework in 1994). A clear pattern emerged from the data: girls' average coursework marks were higher than boys' in every case. In mathematics and combined science boys' marks on the other (non-coursework) components were, on average, higher than girls' marks; in English the girls' average written paper marks remained higher than the boys' average marks, although the difference was less than for the coursework.

Using inter-examination boards' statistics for 1988, 1989 and 1990, Stobart *et al* (1992a) also tested the hypothesis that the improved performance of girls relative to boys, following the introduction of GCSE, was directly related to the weighting and type of coursework required. They ranked subjects in terms of the typical weighting of coursework at that time and discovered that the ranking with English at the top (50% to 100% coursework), history and geography in the middle (typically 30% coursework) followed by biology and chemistry (20% coursework) and mathematics at the bottom (with no compulsory coursework) reflected exactly the gender differences in performance. The only notable exception was French where girls made significant gains without a coursework element (though oral assessment may have had the same effect).

The above research suggests that, for whatever reason, there is a substantial gender effect with respect to coursework. Using 1991 results, Stobart *et al* (1992b) carried out a more detailed and focused study of GCSE mathematics and English to investigate this further. According to Elwood (1995), a member of this team, the study showed that although gender differences were substantial, especially in English, the pattern was present in courses where the coursework element was reduced. Indeed, the gender gap was most pronounced for syllabuses that were *not* 100% assessed by coursework. Moreover, the gap in performance has not subsequently been reduced in parallel with the restriction to a maximum of 40% coursework (half of which is an oral examination) imposed in 1994.

In their later research on A-levels, Elwood and Comber (1996) noted that girls performed slightly better than boys in the coursework element of A-level in English literature, which accounted for a third of the marks. However, the marks on the coursework element tended to be 'bunched'; it was the marks on the examination papers that allowed more 'discrimination' and therefore contributed most to rank order and, hence, overall grades.

Whilst recognising that there is evidence that girls do better than boys at coursework, these researchers argue that the coursework *element* in an examination does not automatically determine overall final grades. Other factors intervene and may be equally important; for example, the weighting given to other elements and the amount of discrimination that each element achieves. These are technical issues to do with the construction of the examination, but there are other factors more closely related to in-school experiences such as teachers' preferences for teaching certain syllabuses and other aspects of pedagogy. For instance, if some teachers have greater confidence in teaching syllabuses with reduced coursework or no coursework at all, they might get better results from both boys and girls than if they had taught a 100% coursework option with less commitment. The reverse might be equally true.

Research by Goulding (1995), about how mathematics teachers in 16 schools reacted to the 20% restriction on mathematics coursework in GCSE after 1994 illustrates how such factors operate in particular contexts. Of particular interest were the attitudes of teachers towards the two examination options (20% coursework or no coursework). She described most of the teachers interviewed as either 'pragmatists' (those who preferred didactic teaching, believing that high grades are achievable without coursework, or who wanted to avoid control difficulties associated with low achievers who had to be pressed to hand coursework in), or 'pedagogues' (those who saw coursework as consonant with their favoured teaching approach). The performance of girls taught by the pedagogues was not always superior to those taught by the pragmatists, although one would expect this to be the case if coursework benefited girls in all circumstances.

Whichever way one chooses to interpret the evidence about course-work and performance, data, arising from a recent project investigating users' perceptions of the GCSE (Bishop *et al*, 1996), indicate that gender is certainly a factor in *perceptions* of coursework. A small but significant percentage of girls perceived coursework more favourably than did boys. A core of lower ability boys was not motivated by coursework, but middle and lower ability girls perceived coursework as giving them a better chance of success. Twenty-three per cent of boys considered coursework to favour girls, whereas only 9% of girls perceived an advantage to themselves. These differences were in stark contrast to the views of teachers, 53% of whom thought there was a difference between boys' and girls' ability to do coursework; no fewer than nine out of ten of this group believed that coursework favoured girls.

- There is a perception, especially among teachers, that coursework favours girls.

- There is some evidence that girls do slightly better than boys on the coursework elements of examinations but this may only marginally affect pupils' overall results because other elements in the examination can be more critical in determining final grades. Schools may select syllabuses with different coursework proportions according to their estimation of their teaching strengths or their perception of the relative confidence and ability of their pupils.

- To be fair to both boys and girls it is likely that a variety of assessment modes should be used so that all pupils have opportunities to produce their best performance.

3.3 ITEM CONTENT, CONTEXT AND STYLE OF RESPONSE

The survey of the Assessment of Performance Unit (APU) between 1978 and 1989 recorded findings in terms of specific task items. A number of the researchers who analysed the APU data have concluded that any gender effect should be considered in relation to a task effect.[3]

Task Content

APU science results showed that girls and boys reacted to the same *content* (what the task was about) differently. More girls would attempt, and perform better on, questions to do with health, nutrition and domestic situations, while boys performed better on items about, cars, buildings and machinery. Both sexes avoided what was outside their 'territory'. In APU design and technology tasks, girls focused on aesthetic and affective aspects whilst boys focused on structural and manufacturing aspects.

- Boys and girls prefer, and perform better on, tasks involving content with which they are especially familiar through direct experience in the home or school.

Item Context

APU surveys also revealed that items set within a *context* (to give them authenticity) elicited different responses from boys and girls. Girls valued the circumstances in which tasks were set and took account of them when framing a solution, whereas boys were more inclined to abstract issues from their context, judging context to be irrelevant. This often disadvantaged girls in mathematicss, but not in design and technology where the evaluation of products in terms of human needs is important.

- Girls value the contexts in which tasks are framed and take account of them in their responses. This can create difficulties for them if this was not what the assessor intended.

Style of Response

The APU English team found that girls prefer to communicate their feelings about things in extended, reflective composition while boys provided episodic, factual and commentative detail. This finding is confirmed by a later study of GCSE English by Punter and Burchell (1996). They found that among the 20 main kinds of response required in GCSE English for examinations and coursework assignments, girls were better than boys in approaching 15 (such as 'writing extended pieces') while boys were only seen as outperforming girls significantly in 'writing argumentatively or factually' and 'interpreting visual materials'.

These responses to writing tasks, which also reflect gender preferences in reading, may account in some measure for patterns of relative performance across subjects and phases of education. The style of girls' reading and writing is valued in English and in the early phases of education, whilst the style of boys' reading and writing is valued in domains like science and, increasingly, in the later phases of education.

- Boys and girls favour different styles of response to assessment items which reflect their writing and reading preferences; these differences may account, in some measure, for differential performance across subjects and phases of education.

By analysing task content, context and style of expression, the APU was able to catalogue tasks which were known to favour one gender. Stobart *et al* (1992b) used the APU framework for task analysis as a starting point for their analysis of examination papers. In line with the APU, this study revealed that girls did better in English when responses involved extended writing, when multiple perspectives were required to achieve good marks and when literary stimulus materials were used. Boys did better when questions required short responses or right/wrong answers and when questions were based on topics which required technical knowledge and expository prose.

An analysis of the content of examination papers confirmed that stimulus material reflected a balance of texts showing examiners' awareness of issues related to gender. However, it was found that only a rather narrow set of literacy skills were sampled: questions focused on characters, their feelings and motivations (areas which the APU had shown girls to be good at). The marking scheme also favoured writing performance over understanding of text. Therefore, more boys' responses than those of girls were found wanting in terms of organisation, style, grammar and spelling.

- There is evidence that issues of gender bias in stimulus materials for GCSE English have been confronted; however, the same attention has not been given to types of task and mark schemes which might account for some of the gender gap.

In mathematics the application of the APU framework to GCSE papers told a different story. Where the APU had noticed large differences between boys and girls (on such topics as rate, ratio, shape and space, where boys outperformed girls), the size of the gap had decreased to the extent that exam papers no longer appeared biased in favour of any one group.

- The papers in GCSE mathematics no longer appear to be biased in favour of any one group, which might account for the comparable performances of boys and girls.

3.4 MARKER BIAS

At school level a small experimental study by Goddard-Spear (1983) has cast doubt on the objectivity of teachers as assessors. Two groups of science teachers were asked to grade a piece of science writing. The group who were told that the writing had been done by a boy graded it more highly than the group who were told it had been done by a girl. The implication of this was that assessors tend to mark the work of boys more highly than the work of girls. The most recent research on A-levels, however, challenges the universality of this finding and also Bradley's (1984) conclusion that markers exhibit a 'centralist tendency' when assessing the work of girls.

According to research from the Associated Examining Board (Baird, 1996), A-level examiners show no evidence of gender bias. Two experiments in 'blind marking' were carried out in A-level English literature and Chemistry (subjects with strong gender-stereotyped images). Twenty-four examiners took part in the study and each was given 30 scripts. The content of each examiner's scripts was identical to the content of every other examiner's scripts but the presentation was altered to see if it had any effect on the marks awarded.[4]

In the experiments each script was available in four forms: male name, male handwriting; male name, female handwriting; female name, male handwriting; female name, female handwriting. One group of examiners was asked to mark the scripts 'blind' (i.e. with names removed) the control group marked them in line with current practice (i.e. with names at the top). None of the examiners was told the purpose of the exercise. The study found that marks were not affected in either English or chemistry by the gender of the name on the script or by the gender style of the handwriting. This suggests that examiners do not possess simplistic stereotypes about male and female performance at A-level.

- Earlier evidence found that the work of women and girls was not judged as favourably as the work of men and boys when the performance was generally very good but attracted leniency when it was poor. More recent evidence, however, suggests that marker bias in relation to gender may have diminished or disappeared, at least in relation to A-level.

---

[1] Keys, Harris and Fernandes (1996).

[2] These recent findings are consistent with work from the 1970s and 1980s (Murphy, 1982) and from the USA (Schmitt *et al,* 1991) and Australia (SSABSA 1993).

[3] Gorman *et al* (1991); Foxman *et al* (1985); DES (1988a,b;1989); Kimbell *et al* (1991).

[4] The researcher had previously confirmed that people who had been shown unnamed scripts were able to guess the sex of the writer from handwriting alone in 70% of cases. Girls tend to have a more rounded handwriting style; boys' writing is freer and more untidy.

4 SINGLE-SEX OR CO-EDUCATION? THE EFFECTS OF SCHOOLS ON PUPILS' PERFORMANCES

The question of whether pupils make greater progress when they are educated in mixed or single-sex schools has always been a controversial one and the publication of annual tables on schools' examination results has certainly fuelled the discussion. Debates have focused on two fronts:

First, a number of commentators have noted the relatively prominent positions of all-girls schools in the performance tables.[1] To what extent, they have asked, has their performance been due to the single-sex basis of their organisation?

Second, a very large number of mixed schools, when breaking down their results separately by gender, have noted that their girls have outperformed their boys – sometimes by a considerable margin.[2]

This chapter considers the results of research on school effectiveness; the specific effects of single-sex and co-educational schools on pupil performance and subject choices; and then, more generally, the impact secondary schools have on the progress of boys and girls.

4.1 RESEARCH ON SCHOOL EFFECTIVENESS

A recent OFSTED analysis looked at both the comprehensive and selective sectors of the educational system. It showed that in 1995 girls outperformed boys in both sectors. Amongst comprehensive schools around 8–10% more girls got over the five or more A*–C hurdle than boys, whether one was looking at mixed or single-sex comprehensives (see Figure 4.1). Similar results were found in the selective system. Girls in grammar and other selective schools did a little better than boys; and girls in secondary modern schools did substantially better than their male counterparts. Such differences in performance need to be assessed cautiously, however. As another official report emerging around the same time put it: 'Numerous uncertainties need to be taken into account in considering the respective merits of mixed and single-sex schools in achieving high standards' (OFSTED/EOC, 1996, p.25).

Figure 4.1

Percentage of 15+-year-old pupils achieving 5+ A*–C Grades at GCSE 1995

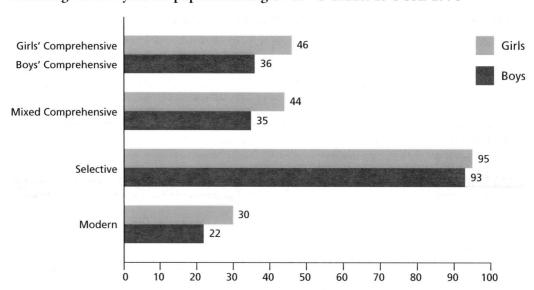

Source: OFSTED analysis (1996)

Research on school effectiveness has found that schools which manage, by one means or another, to create a 'distinctive' ethos seem to do well on conventional criteria of educational performance. The most obvious reason why a school might achieve such 'distinctiveness' is because it has brought together pupils from similar backgrounds. 'Similarity' in this context might result from decisions to recruit pupils:

- of the same gender;

- whose parents were generally more supportive of education;

- from groups with higher *prior* attainments; or

- from groups of the same religious persuasion or sharing some other set of values and beliefs.

All four of these factors are known to be associated with higher levels of performance. The challenge is to try to disentangle them from: (a) the type of school organisation (single-sex or mixed) to see if school type still 'makes a difference' when other relevant factors have been taken into account; and (b) whether any other 'distinctiveness' may result over and above that brought about by the grouping together of pupils from similar backgrounds.

There are many problems in this kind of research which need to be borne in mind when looking at the evidence. In particular, it has often proved difficult for researchers to ensure that like is truly being compared with like. Common stumbling blocks have included:

- the absence of adequate measures on pupils' prior attainment;

- the number of 'distinctive' schools being too small for proper statistical analysis;

- the difficulty of finding pupils who are 'really similar' in the different types of institution; and

- the use of statistical methods which have been too crude to tease out differences in effectiveness.

The number of studies which meet all these various criteria is very small indeed.[3] Furthermore, only a handful have been conducted in school systems which are sufficiently like the English one to make generalisations worth while. This review of the evidence is consequently confined largely to those studies where the various considerations outlined above have, by one means or another, been taken into account.

4.2 STUDIES OF SINGLE-SEX AND CO-EDUCATIONAL SCHOOLING

The Cases of England and Ireland

To date, there has been only one major national study of English schools which has looked at the single-sex issue in any detail (Steedman, 1985). It was based on a cohort of pupils who were born in 1958 and who passed through secondary schools during the mid-seventies.

This research showed that pupils in single-sex schools were already performing at somewhat higher levels in terms of reading, mathematics and general attainment *before* they entered secondary schools. It also showed that just over a half of all the girls entering girls-only schools and just under half the boys entering boys-only schools were from non-manual backgrounds. By contrast under a third of both girls and boys entering mixed schools were from non-manual backgrounds. No research since then has indicated patterns of intake markedly at variance with these general findings.

Steedman's findings 'suggest(ed) that very little in their examination results was explained by whether schools were mixed or single sex, *once allowance had been made for differences in (their) intakes*' (1985, p.98, our emphasis).

Steedman's study is now rather dated and relates to a period when the overall performance levels of boys and girls in examinations at the end of compulsory study were on a more even footing.[4] Several more recent studies of performance at GCSE from researchers at the London Institute of Education have also looked at this issue, but only in passing; all have found small differences favouring girls-only schools (see, for example, Nuttall *et al*, 1989). Unfortunately all but the most recent study (Thomas *et al*, 1994) have suffered from the limitation that they were confined to *examination candidates*, rather than all the pupils in the school. Thomas' study concluded that there were no statistically significant differences between mixed and single-sex schools in performance.

Daly (1996) has recently reported the results of two surveys in Northern Ireland conducted during the 1980s.[5] In the first survey, he concluded that whether the school was of mixed- or single-sex was not significant, 'although there was a *suggestion* of a slight disadvantage associated with co-educational schooling'. In the second survey Daly commented more forcibly on the absence of a significant 'school sex-composition effect', referring to it as a 'notable finding'.

By far the most comprehensive attempt to examine the mixed/single-sex issue has been completed in the Republic of Ireland (Hannan *et al*, 1996). The data from this study are a good deal more contemporary and the sample sizes much larger. And, whereas in most research studies single-sex schools have been educating a small and potentially 'distinctive' minority, in the Irish study their pupils made up somewhere approaching half of the whole population of schools.[6] As in many other OECD countries, more girls in Ireland sit the leaving examinations; they also perform better in them than boys (OECD, 1995). However, as elsewhere, 'girls remain significantly under-represented in mathematical, scientific and technical subject areas' (Hannan *et al*, 1996, p.4).

Hannan and colleagues concluded, in relation to pupils' performance in the Junior Certificate (aged around 14), that 'most of the difference in performance between co-educational and single-sex schools was, in fact, due to differences in the social background and ability of their pupil intakes' (1996, p.196). They reached a similar conclusion in relation to pupils' performance on the Leaving Certificate (aged around 16) as well. 'Schools differed significantly from one another in average performance, but this was primarily because of the type of pupils attending them, and the way in which pupils were allocated to classes, not whether they were co-educational or single-sex' (1996, p.197).

Most studies have confined themselves to measures of academic outcomes. This one, however, also looked at aspects of pupils' personal and social development as well as the stress levels they experienced. In general terms they found that pupils in co-educational schools had a 'more positive view of their schools' impact on their personal/social development than pupils in single-sex schools' but such differences were not reflected to the same extent in more objective measures. 'Being in a co-ed school seemed to make boys more self-critical but girls were less confident and had a lower sense of control than boys, no matter what kind of school they attended' (1996, p.199). Furthermore, whilst girls reported much higher levels of stress than boys, stress did not appear to be affected by the type of school attended.

> • The apparently superior performance of single-sex (and especially girls-only) institutions in terms of overall measures of examination results has been largely due to the initially superior performance of the pupils entering these schools. When the different nature of the intakes to the schools has been taken into account the differences usually disappear.

Studies in Other Societies

Whilst there are some difficulties in interpreting the studies described above they have the advantage of being based on systems which have broadly comparable school leaving examinations. Studies of the single-sex/co-educational issue from North America and Australia, for example, present additional difficulties of interpretation. The broad thrust of the evidence from the USA, has tended towards the view that single-sex schooling is more effective for both girls and boys (Riordan, 1990). However, the methodological inadequacies of many of the available studies must be remembered. In one of the larger ones, based on the 'High School and Beyond' national survey, Lee and Bryk (1986) reported that single-sex schools were more effective. However, their single-sex schools were also exclusively Catholic schools, another factor which the same study suggested had positive influences on pupils' attainments. Furthermore, their conclusions have been challenged by other researchers (see Marsh, 1989).

Meanwhile in Australia similar debates continue without any conclusive patterns emerging. There has been a marked decline in the overall number of single-sex girls' schools in the public sector and the pattern has varied quite considerably from one state to the next (Gill,1988). As a fairly recent Australian review commented: 'research on achievement effects has established no clear superiority of either co-educational or single-sex schooling for girls, once other factors are controlled for' (Yates, 1993, p.94).

- A small number of studies in other societies seem to suggest that girls-only institutions retain a very modest edge in performance, even when some major differences in the nature of their intakes have been taken into account. It is difficult to tell whether this advantage results from unmeasured aspects of their intakes, which the researchers have simply failed to take into account, or from the particular ways in which they are organised and teach.

General Trends Across the Studies

There are tentative signs that some differences between the outcomes of single-sex schools and mixed schools still remain after some of the key characteristics of the intakes have been taken into account. These differences seem to be relatively modest but they suggest that the search to establish what is 'distinctive' about single-sex institutions (and especially girls' schools) needs to continue. Have they, for example, succeeded in:

- generating an ethos that is *especially* focused on academic performance?

- adopting teaching methods which are more sensitive to the differences between boys and girls?

- finding some other ways of enhancing the performance of their pupils?

The most striking differences between boys and girls, as shown in Chapter 1, relate to take-up in specific subjects, notably at A-level. To what extent might the type of school attended have affected their decisions about what to study? Again, at first glance, there would appear to be some notable differences. Table 4.1 shows that there was differential take-up in a variety of subjects according to whether the student had previously attended a mixed or single-sex school. Closer inspection of these figures, however, suggests quite complicated patterns which varied from subject to subject.

Girls from girls' schools were more likely to study mathematics or physical sciences at A-level than girls from mixed schools; there were no differences between the two types of schools with respect to A-levels in the life sciences. On the other hand it was boys from mixed schools who were more likely to study mathematics and physical sciences than boys from boys' schools, although this pattern was slightly reversed in the life sciences. Overall boys seemed equally likely to take some science or mathematics course in either type of school whereas amongst girls slightly more did so in girls-only schools (Cheng *et al*, 1995). There were also some differences in other subjects. The most striking difference was the virtual avoidance of modern languages by boys in mixed schools (8% compared with 23% in boys' schools); the differences for girls were by no means so striking (see Table 4.1).

Cheng *et al* (1995) considered how influential the type of school was when compared with other factors. They found that by far the most important predictor of subject choice was how well a student had performed in the same (or related) subjects at GCSE. Furthermore, when they took account of such prior performance, the results proved rather surprising. They found that boys were 'much more likely than girls from all-girls' schools in year 11 to do physical sciences, whether they were from all-boys' schools or from mixed schools'. At the same time, and very much contrary to what they had expected from the debates, they discovered that 'girls from mixed schools also appeared to be more likely to take physical sciences than girls from single-sex schools, although the effect was on the margin of statistical significance'. There were similar findings for the take-up of mathematics.

Table 4.1

GCE A-level subjects by type of school attended at year 11 and gender

	Boys from boys' schools (%)	Girls from girls' schools (%)	Boys from mixed schools (%)	Girls from mixed schools (%)	Total (%)
Mathematics & Science					
Mathematics	42	26	46	21	32
Physical Sciences	39	25	48	19	32
Life Sciences	19	25	16	26	21
(Any sciences and/or maths)	(55)	(43)	(56)	(39)	(48)
Other subjects					
English	28	43	22	49	36
Social Sciences & Humanities	65	65	61	69	65
Modern Languages	23	28	8	25	19
Creative Arts	13	23	15	22	18
Technology	7	2	9	1	5
'Applied' subjects (Business Studies, etc.)	8	10	10	12	10
Classics	7	7	1	2	3

Source: Cheng *et al*, 1995, p.11

In the life sciences there were 'no significant differences (in take-up)…between girls from single-sex schools and boys from either single-sex or mixed schools. However, as with the physical sciences and mathematics…girls from mixed schools were more likely to choose this subject than their counterparts from all-girls schools'.[7]

The researchers concluded that what students had studied at GCSE, and how well they had done in their various subjects, dominated decisions about A-level choices. Girls who did well in the physical sciences and mathematics at GCSE were generally more likely to proceed to these subjects at A-level. The apparent superiority of girls-only schools was basically attributable to their having more able intakes who then went on to perform well in public examinations.

- Pupils in single-sex and co-educational schools make somewhat different choices about what to study at A-level. In particular, girls in girls-only schools seem more likely to study some mathematics or physical sciences. By contrast, boys in mixed schools seem to avoid modern languages.

- The main determinant of which subjects pupils choose to study for A-level appears to be how well they have previously performed in the subject. The different patterns of choice between types of school largely disappear when prior performance in the subjects is taken into account.

Investigation of differences in subject take-up is hampered by the same kinds of methodological flaws noted earlier. It is difficult to ensure that like is really being compared with like. Nonetheless, there do seem to be some general trends in the various analyses from other countries.

Looking at participation in science courses in Northern Ireland, for example, Daly (1995) concluded that 'attendance at single-sex schools did not appear to confer participation or attainment advantages on pupils'. He reached the same conclusions about mathematics for the same samples (Daly and Shuttleworth, 1995). Findings from the recent study in Eire paint a largely similar picture; differences in participation and performance in science and mathematics between pupils attending different types of school diminished when the nature of their intakes was taken into account, although girls-only schools did retain an edge (Hannan *et al*, 1996).[8]

Lee and Bryk (1986) mention a number of potentially important reasons why single-sex institutions *might* retain a residual edge in relation to subject choice. Teachers are more likely to be of the same sex, thereby possibly providing more appropriate adult role models; members of single-sex schools tend to share other values in common (in Lee's and Bryk's case a commitment to Catholicism); and, for one reason or another, many such schools may be in a position to attract more effective staff. Furthermore, some of these factors may be mutually reinforcing. As Lee and Bryk put it: 'It is *quite plausible* that single-sex school organisation could produce not only a positive environment for learning but also a positive environment for teaching' (1986, p.393, our emphasis). Such considerations would certainly help to explain why the differences were occurring but also suggest it would be quite difficult to reproduce them in other settings.

4.4 GENDER-RELATED DIFFERENTIALS IN EFFECTIVENESS BETWEEN SCHOOLS

Attempts over the last two decades to show that one system of school organisation is more effective than another have not yielded much fruit. As a result researchers have turned their attention to the factors which might make one school more effective than another. To date, however, very little of this work has focused directly on the question of whether some schools are more effective for one sex or the other. We therefore commissioned an analysis of the evidence from over 30 schools in one LEA.

Figure 4.2 shows the recent position for the schools in one local authority which performs around the national average (based on Jesson, 1997). This LEA was chosen because it was one of a still relatively small number of LEAs which have been undertaking value-added analyses over a number of years in a form which allows the individual differences in achievement of boys and girls to be disentangled.[9] The availability of data-bases which link individual pupils' performances at 11 and 16 is essential for this kind of analysis.

The red line shows the average number of 'good' (A*–C) grades obtained by girls in each school at GCSE; the black line shows the same information for boys in the same schools. The vertical distance between the two points on the graph for each school is the 'gender gap' in performance. Thus, in School 1 (on the very left hand side of the figure) the boys in the school were averaging around one and a half 'good' (A*–C) passes and the girls somewhere over two. In School 33 (on the righthand side of the figure) the boys were averaging around six 'good' passes, whilst the girls were averaging closer to seven.

In the majority of schools the performance of the girls was higher than that of the boys. In a small minority of schools, however, this was not the case; the performance of the two groups was equal (schools numbered 6, 9 and 22) or the boys were performing *slightly* better (numbers 11 and 13).

When differences in the prior attainments of the intakes to the schools have been taken into account, the picture changes (see Figure 4.3). Nonetheless, girls were still outperforming boys by an average of just under one 'higher' grade pass each. In School 1, for example, the girls were achieving just over half a 'good' pass *less* than predicted from knowledge of their performance at 11; the boys, however, were achieving around one and a half 'good' passes *less* than predicted. In taking account of differences in prior attainment the gap actually widened still further.

Figure 4.2

Examination results for girls and boys in mixed schools: performance data published in 1996

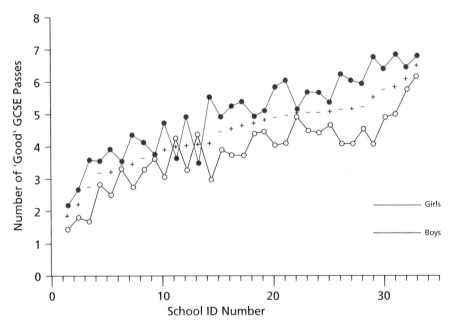

Note: The schools have been ranked along the horizontal scale from the one with the lowest *overall* performance (No.1) to the highest *overall* performance. For each school the average scores of their boys and their girls are recorded separately on the vertical scale.

The overall analysis confirmed the 'effectiveness' for boys of four of the schools listed above (all except 22) and identified a further two where this was also the case (numbers 4 and 31). However, it also revealed several more schools where the gap appeared to be wider than the 'raw' results had suggested. The overall conclusion to be drawn from this analysis is a striking one.

> • Some four out of five schools in this one LEA would seem to have been 'more effective' for their girls than for their boys. Only a small minority of schools appear to have found ways of being equally effective for both sexes.

It is not clear from the data available for this analysis whether the position in this small minority of schools resulted from *deliberate* efforts on the part of these schools to address the gender problem.

Figure 4.3

Examination results for girls and boys in mixed schools: difference between actual and predicted performance in each school

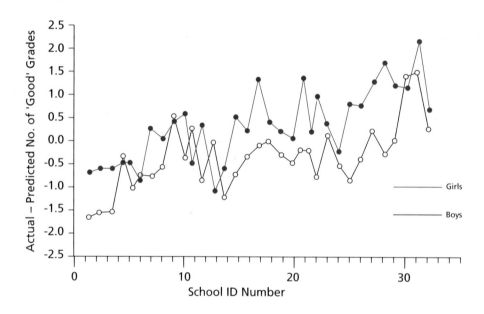

The number of studies, in this country or elsewhere, which focus directly on the specific effects of schools on gender differences is very limited. Experience suggests that it would be unwise to generalise too widely on such a slender basis. Replications in other LEAs are required. However, the almost total absence of schools in this LEA where boys were making greater progress than girls suggests that some alternative strategies for establishing what might work are likely to be required. Simply studying the 'naturally-occurring' variation is unlikely to be enough. In such situations there is another approach which can pay dividends. This is to focus on the efforts of those institutions which have taken *very deliberate steps* to tackle the problem (see Chapter 7 below).

> • More research is needed on school effectiveness related to some of the factors which affect schools' progress in reducing gender gaps at GCSE and A-level and in relation to national assessments.

[1] Some of these perceptions are discussed more fully in Smithers and Robinson (1995).

[2] Previous concerns about performance have been signalled in several earlier quotations; see Deem (1984) for a fuller discussion. For insights about how parents conceptualise the 'distinctiveness' of single-sex schools, particularly when choosing a secondary school for girls, see David, West and Ribbens (1994).

[3] Hardly any have had good data on pupils' prior attainments.

[4] See Chapter 1, Figure 1.3.

[5] The first of these studies was rather small (only 21 schools) but contained a good measure of prior attainment. The second was rather larger (over 150 schools) but with a poorer control for prior attainment.

[6] It should perhaps be remembered that, within the Irish context, single-sex schools are almost all Catholic schools.

[7] Cheng *et al* (1995), pp.19-21.

[8] Dutch and Australian studies have reached the same kinds of conclusions: Bosker and Dekkers (1994), Daly, Ainley and Robinson (1996).

[9] The Annual Report of the Chief Inspector for 1995/96 remarks that: 'Several LEAs are concerned about differences in the achievement of boys and girls...but few are yet monitoring and analysing pupil achievement or attendance in a systematic way.' (HMSO, 1997, p.43).

PART 3

DEVELOPMENTAL AND CULTURAL PROCESSES

5 MALE AND FEMALE DEVELOPMENT AND SCHOOL CAREERS

Girls' and boys' performance on different modes of assessment and teaching styles (identified in Chapter 3) appear to have less to do with the type of school attended and more to do with the ways in which young people develop in them. This section considers recent research on pupil development during the years of compulsory schooling.

Research in this framework addresses the following questions:

First, are differences in the development of male and female children primarily biological in origin, or are they the result of social influences?

Second, do differences in the socialisation of boys and girls lead to differences in motivational processes, which in turn produce differential performance?

Third, do values about gender affect teachers' assessments of pupils' behaviour and learning needs?

5.1 BIOLOGICAL EXPLANATIONS OF EDUCATIONAL PERFORMANCE

Despite a resurgence of interest in biological explanations for psychological phenomena in recent years, it is now generally acknowledged that such explanations are unlikely to provide an adequate account of gender differences in academic performance, and especially of changes in the patterns of male and female achievement. Having reviewed the evidence, Halpern (1992) commented:

> 'When it comes to biological explanations for cognitive processes, we still have more questions than answers.'[1]

Differences between male and female performance on tests of verbal and spatial ability have been recorded but the results do not fit into a simple pattern of sex differences. This is consistent with the fact that no clear sex differences in the size (adjusted for body weight), weight, or complexity of male and female brains has been demonstrated.

Nevertheless, at the extremes of performance, biological influences may be important, although even here sex differences are often only one factor in a complex situation. For example, cerebral lateralisation (as indicated by being left- or right-handed) has been demonstrated to combine with sex differences in a number of ways.

Among high-ability students left-handed boys perform better on tests of verbal abilities but less well on tests of spatial abilities than right-handed boys. The opposite pattern was found for girls. Among boys with extremely low abilities there is a high number who are left-handed – yet there are also large numbers of left-handed pupils at the high-ability end of the distribution. As Halpern notes, it is difficult to account for such complex patterns of results with theories which rest upon a simple dichotomy which contrasts nature with nurture.

Language acquisition, especially in the early years, may also be influenced by biological processes. Girls have been observed to acquire some language concepts (such as the passive voice) earlier than boys; this may be due to a female advantage in maturation and not just family conversational patterns in favour of girls (Halpern, 1992).

It has been difficult to account for these cognitive differences between the sexes with a model of biological determination. The pattern of sex differences is often unstable across cultures, across time within cultures, and also through time in the development of children.

- Even if biology sets limits to human abilities, there is no certainty about what these limits might be, nor whether they are different for men and women.

5.2 SOCIAL AND PSYCHOLOGICAL EXPLANATIONS

Researchers have experienced difficulty in generating explanations in terms of social and psychological processes which command wide support. A number of different theories and research methods have been developed, which creates difficulties in relating their findings.

Some general themes can be identified. Differential patterns of interaction of very young children with caregivers can be observed,[2] reflecting different expectations and attitudes towards male and female children. These expectations set in train different patterns of growth and development for boys and girls. There is also abundant evidence that children acquire different patterns of gender identity in the pre-school years,[3] although how such differences influence performance during the school years remains open to discussion.

Gender Differences in Motivation

The concept of self-esteem has long been held to have important consequences for motivation and learning and to be the mediating variable between school practice and academic performance. A key distinction is made between *general* self-esteem or self-confidence and *specific* self-esteem or confidence in relation to performance in a particular activity, subject, or area of work. Young people can have low levels of confidence in relation to school work, but have high general levels of self-esteem in relation to themselves. The opposite can also be true.

From the point of view of gender differences in performance, two broad research questions need to be addressed:

(a) do girls and boys differ in their levels of self-esteem in ways which are linked to differences in performance?

(b) are gender influences in school practices linked to different levels of self-esteem for girls and boys?

Until recently it has been argued that, compared with boys, girls experience low levels of self-esteem, resulting in lower levels of academic performance. The perceived deficit has led to the framing of national policies for raising girls' self-esteem such as the Commonwealth Schools Commission's programmes (1975, 1984) in Australia. Yet, as recent re-assessments have suggested, evidence for a lack of self-esteem in girls is 'surprisingly thin' (Renshaw, 1990, p.18).

> • Two of the major reviews of research into sex differences both reported little or no evidence for differences in overall self-esteem.[4]

Kenway's and Willis's (1990) comprehensive collection of critiques of this literature is forceful in the evidence it brings to bear. Low self-esteem has often been put forward as an explanation for the poor performance not only of girls, but also of children from ethnic minority and socially disadvantaged groups. The supporting research has been open to serious methodological criticism, however, both about the sampling techniques employed and the reliability and validity of the test measures used.[5]

Further, careful scrutiny of general self-esteem tests suggests that high scoring results appear to be positively correlated with masculinity. Skaalvick's (1986) review of ten studies which had adequately-described samples and were methodologically sound found that in all ten studies when children were asked simply how 'proud, pleased or satisfied they are with themselves', boys scored higher than girls. He concluded that these tests may be encouraging boys to display exaggerated feelings of pride, confident perceptions of themselves and their abilities and a certain amount of bravura. In contrast, girls, having been taught to be modestly feminine, may not wish to answer assuredly such questions about their abilities. The results may therefore be manufactured by the test and may only be indicating the level of 'masculinity'.

Renshaw (1990), after reviewing the available international evidence on gender and self-esteem, concludes that:

> 'The evidence on the level of girls' self-esteem suggests that only a fraction of girls (perhaps 10%) have very low self-esteem, and there is no evidence that schools have a progressively detrimental influence on girls' self-esteem...Throughout the whole school age group, boys' and girls' total self-esteem is remarkably similar.'

Renshaw's review suggests that there are differences between girls and boys in *specific* aspects of self-esteem, and that 'these differences parallel domains that have been more clearly sex role stereotyped' (p. 31). The greater propensity for girls to develop what Dweck and her American colleagues[6] called 'learned helplessness' relates to Renshaw's findings. In this case self-esteem is a consequence of children identifying the *causes* of their successes and failures in particular school tasks in a particular way. *High* self-esteem is defined as the persistence which some children demonstrate in the face of initial failure and their confidence that the goals of the task can be successfully achieved. When failure is repeatedly attributed to a deficiency in the self, children can come to perceive failure as inevitable. This pattern of chronic low self-esteem is described as 'learned helplessness'.

A recent British study[7] of A-level students found that girls in traditional male subjects seemed to lack confidence in their academic work in spite of their success. The authors argue that:

> 'the impression of girls' greater uncertainty is reinforced by the fact that the girls were better qualified than the boys, yet sometimes responded in a way characteristic of the less able group.' (p.50)

Girls, in contrast with boys, spent longer talking to advisers, mentioned more difficulties and appeared to be more worried about whether they were coping with the demands of the course. This could imply that they are better learners or it could imply a deep-seated insecurity about their abilities.

Dweck and her colleagues have related the differential rate of learned helplessness among girls and boys to differences in the types and amount of feedback given to children by their teachers. Boys were frequently criticised for such things as lack of neatness in their work, while girls, although criticised less overall, were more frequently criticised about intellectual aspects of their classroom performance.

Researchers have tended to assume that the direction of causality is from self-esteem to achievement. Renshaw's review, however, suggests that although there is positive correlation between the two variables[8] it has typically been rather low. No particular inference can be drawn, therefore, that changes in self-esteem *precede* changes in achievement. Success in educational performance can raise self-esteem (either specifically or generally).

Further, the correlation between self-esteem and achievement has been similar for boys and girls. As Renshaw comments:

> 'The implication of such a pattern highlights the importance of examining the quality of teaching and resource allocation for girls rather than focusing on presumed deficits within individual girls.' (p.31)

Shaw's (1995) work offers a new approach to the study of motivation and its relationship to gender by introducing emotion as a central theme in children's experience of learning. She suggests that it would be fruitful to look more carefully at the emotional development of boys and girls in the family and how this might generate different forms of anxiety around gender identities. Her argument is complex, but it can be illustrated through her consideration of boys' development. She, along with others, suggests that the process of boys' separation from their mothers is achieved through the classifying of activities, behaviours and spheres of work into male and female. Boys who are anxious about their masculine identities distance themselves from feminine activities, making sure that other boys do so as well. They are more likely to make distinctions between 'male' science, reason, abstract and intellectual knowledge and 'female' art, emotion, practical knowledge and feelings (see Section 2.2 above). These early experiences, especially if reinforced by the school, may account for boys' lower performance in English and other 'feminine' subjects, or their opinion of schoolwork generally as effeminate. The question Shaw wants explored is how far differences in male and female academic performance are due to the different anxieties boys and girls might have about their gender identities. By 'using anxiety almost as a form of energy' (p.144), are schools increasing boys' insecurity about their masculinity making them perhaps even more likely to polarise the sexes?

- Further research is needed to explore the developmental antecedents of male and [...] consequences for academic performance.

GENDER VALUES IN SCHOOL CULTURES

The school has traditionally been viewed as one of the principal socialising agents in children's lives. Recent research suggests that the messages transmitted through curriculum texts are either more complex than originally thought or have been modified through gender initiatives.[9] Thus, while there may still be gender stereotyping in curriculum materials, the shifting pattern of performance between the sexes described in Chapter 1 suggests that gender bias in the curriculum cannot be seen as the only cause of high or low achievement. More attention is currently being paid to teachers' gender values and how they might come into play in shaping and responding to pupils' attitudes to schooling and their patterns of behaviour.

Teachers' Gender Values

Surveys of teachers' attitudes to equal opportunities issues in the mid-1980s suggested that science teachers and male teachers were more likely to be hostile to promoting gender equality, while female teachers and humanities teachers were reported to be more positive (Goddard-Spear, 1985). Since then there have been few surveys, possibly because respondents are now thought to be too familiar with what would constitute the 'right answers'.

Instead, in-depth qualitative studies have investigated the relationship between teachers' understanding of gender issues and their classroom practice. Recent investigations in both the UK and Australia[10] suggest that primary teachers who interpret child-centred approaches to include an expectation of 'normal stages of development' may endorse strong gender differences, especially male aggression and female passivity. Their training may have encouraged them to expect 'boys to be boys' and 'girls to be girls' and thus to accept that boys will express themselves more aggressively and boisterously.

Some of the most informative research on the influence of teachers' attitudes has come from case studies of individual schools which have suggested that [...] ntinuing areas of concern about the nature and impact of boys' and [...] th teachers. Abraham's (1995) research, for [...] stances on sex roles 'strongly influence their specific [...] choice of curriculum materials' (p.136). More signific[...]

'conflicting gender value systems can also give rise to polarisation both between pupils and between teachers and pupils. Sometimes this has an impact on the extent and the nature of anti-school behaviour that can, in turn, have an impact on academic performance.' (p.135)

Research has generally found that girls report greater levels of enjoyment at school than boys; this is also expressed in girls' reporting stronger levels of liking for both academic and non-academic aspects of school life (Lightbody *et al*, 1996). Girls are also more likely to find opportunities for self-expression and for developing self-confidence.[11] Graham's (1994) survey of 4,000 pupils found that after a falling off in the *rapport* between students and their school between years 7 and 9, boys showed less capacity than girls to improve their commitment to school after year 9. Pupils explained the differences by referring to the different ways teachers behaved towards male and female pupils and the generalised expectations of the school.

Similarly Cullingford's (1993) interviews with year 7 children indicate that both girls and boys are sensitive to gender biases in the ways teachers treat pupils. Boys, in particular, resent the unfairness they perceive when they are picked on by teachers for doing the same things as girls – as if teachers expect boys to be noisier and more badly behaved.[12]

- There is evidence that teachers' gender role in shaping pupils' perceptions of, and reactions to, school.

Although the causal connection between the quality of pupil interactions with teachers (and other pupils) and their academic performance is not clearly established, recent research points to the importance of exploring more systematically pupils' negative experiences of school such as bullying and harassment, and poor academic achievement. The authors of one study of bullying found that being bullied or being a bully can 'have a wearing effect on victims causing health problems as well as affecting pupils' school work' (Williams *et al*, 1996).

One problem in making this connection between harassment and performance is that it is notoriously hard to discover the extent of bullying in schools: school inspections have found 'little evidence of bullying' and most schools are reported to have sound policies for dealing with bullying and treating incidents of bullying seriously' (H.M. Chief Inspector's Annual Report, 1995–6, p.22). However, a number of studies in the last few years, which used self-reporting surveys with clear definitions of bullying or which used open-ended questionnaires and interviews (with, for example, school nurses)[13] suggest that a high proportion of children in the UK have been bullied (or teased) at some time in their school life.[14]

Bullying seems particularly high[15] in primary schools at an age when gender identities are still being formed. Whitney and Smith (1993) found that more than one in four primary pupils in Sheffield (compared with one in ten secondary pupils) reported being bullied 'sometimes' in a term. MacLeod's and Morris's recent survey for Childline (1996), using open-ended questions, found that these figures rose to 50% of primary and 27% of secondary children in London and the South East, who said they were bullied in school during the last year. Most bullying is reported happening in primary school playgrounds and in secondary school classrooms. The rates of reported bullying have not been found to correlate with school size, class size or ethnic mix, but have been found to vary with year, gender and school location (e.g. areas of social disadvantage) (Whitney and Smith, 1993).

Gender has been implicated in bullying because boys tend to bully more than girls and because male and female bullying as an activity tends to vary, with boys more likely to produce behaviour that is physical, violent or aggressive, and girls more likely to use more verbal and indirect (e.g. social exclusion) methods. Boys tend to bully boys and girls, whilst girls tend to only bully other girls (Whitney and Smith, 1993).

Balding *et al* (1996) found that more secondary girls than boys fear going to school, even though in secondary schools boys are more likely to be victims and to experience physical violence (Pitts and Smith, 1995). Girls reported receiving dirty looks and having stories told against them. Non-white pupils also reported being victimised.

Such events may be interpreted by teachers (and parents) as a consequence of a 'natural' developmental process in which, for example, 'boys will be boys' (Askew, 1989; Keise, 1991). Bullying may not be recognised in the context of pressures on boys to conform to male stereotypes, particularly in terms of their developing sexual identities. Abusive language used by pupils can have strong sexual connotations that can undermine girls' self-confidence and divert their attention away from their academic work (Lees, 1986); it can also seriously undermine the wellbeing of boys whose masculinity is being challenged (Epstein 1997). As Wolpe (1989) argued:

> 'One of the causal factors in the low level of achievement in academic terms appears to be the effect of erupting sexuality in pupils' lives.' (p.97)

New studies suggest that 'disengaged' male pupils who are underachieving appear to be more likely to be involved in bullying incidents, to feel that teachers are unaware of the amount of bullying they endure, and to feel, on the one hand, under pressure from their immediate friends not to achieve and, on the other, under pressure from their teachers not to be an annoyance to the achieving pupils (Chaplain, Miles and Rudduck, 1994).

- More research is needed on the effects of bullying and harassment on male and female performance.

Pupil Behaviour and Special Needs

New links are now being made between the assessment of pupil needs and male and female patterns of performance, and the role that the gender values of the school and teachers might play in creating gender differences in outcomes. In 1975, Rutter suggested that the over-representation of boys in anti-school disruptive student groups was related to the emphasis by schools on assertiveness and aggression as positive masculine characteristics. Teachers may unintentionally reinforce male assertiveness as well as react to its display.

National data for 1993–4 suggest that male and female African–Caribbean pupils are being excluded four times as often as would be predicted by their numbers in the secondary school population and the equivalent of 12 times as often in primary schools.[16]

Conflicts between teachers and black pupils can arise if there are misunderstandings about, for example, cultural values and behaviour (such as body movements, posture, gestures, etc.). Investigations of black pupils' experiences of schooling suggest that there is considerable tension around appropriate behaviour in school which, if it is not checked, can lead to low teacher expectations of such pupils' academic abilities (Gillborn, 1990; Wright, 1986, 1992). The OFSTED report, *Exclusions from Secondary Schools* (1996), presents examples of a group of African–Caribbean pupils (12 boys and three girls) who were of average or above average ability, but were described by schools as 'underachieving'. This pattern seems particularly, although not exclusively relevant to black *male* pupils. Mac an Ghaill (1988) found in his in-depth study of a Midlands comprehensive school that racial confrontations resulted from teachers using stereotypes of the African–Caribbean and Asian communities and youth as a way of explaining pupil behaviour. Black pupils, particularly boys, were defined as 'problems' – an image that prevented them from being perceived as 'young, gifted and black'.

Gender confrontations were also found to be associated with pupil disaffection and high exclusion rates amongst African–Caribbean male youth by a more recent study of a London comprehensive. Sewell's (1997) study suggests that contemporary styles of masculinity associated with young African–Caribbean male youth may be the focal point of such teacher–pupil conflict. African–Caribbean girls, in contrast, have said that they experience less trouble than boys, perhaps because they respond to such racial conflicts with different, less visible strategies (Mac an Ghaill, 1988; Mirza, 1992). This may account for some of the differences in African–Caribbean male and female pupils' performance (see Section 6.3 below).

Statementing procedures can also differentiate between girls and boys, both in terms of the number of pupils statemented and the types of needs being identified.[17] Boys tend to outnumber girls in all categories of difficulty,[18] but especially in social, emotional and behavioural difficulties. Tomlinson (1982, 1988) calls these difficulties 'non-normative' since cultural and social factors are likely to be called into play by professionals. Working-class boys are more likely to be identified in these categories, whilst middle-class boys have been found to predominate in non-stigmatised groups – for example, specific learning difficulties such as dyslexia (Riddell, 1996; Riddell *et al*, 1994).

The interpretation of pupil needs, and the language used by teachers and educational psychologists to describe the reason for statementing can reflect stereotypical understandings about gender, but also about race and class. Hill's (1994) study of 50 statements in Sheffield and Rotherham, for example, found that boys tended to be described as more academically able than girls, but also as aggressive, disruptive, having limited concentration, withdrawn and violent; girls were described as less academic than boys and as daydreamers, passive, socially vulnerable and 'strange'. As Riddell points out, we do not know whether such descriptions accorded with pupils' actual classroom behaviour.

The effect of gender on provision of extra support in school is equally complex. Important new research suggests, for example, that boys may receive more support when in difficulties than girls in mainstream junior schools.[19] Significant gender differences have been found by Daniels *et al* (1996) in the number of female and male children receiving support, and the types of special provision. Boys appeared to be given more help in terms of time, and more prestigious and expensive forms of support (e.g. literacy support, primary helper time). The only form of provision girls received more of than boys was help from volunteers (p.7).

Table 5.1

Race by Gender by SEN in one LEA

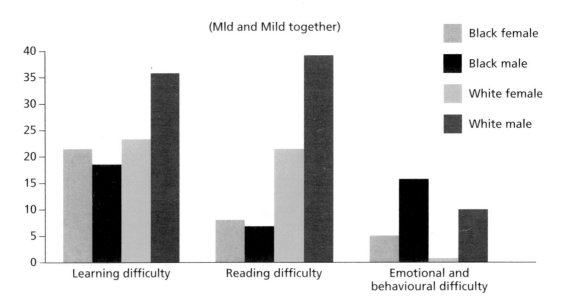

In 21 junior schools in one inner city LEA the researchers found that gender equality only seemed to occur in relation to those with mild learning difficulties. In the other SEN categories there were 'worrying imbalances' in the gender and racial backgrounds of children. Table 5.1 above shows that within both black[20] and white groups gender differences were greatest in the categories of emotional and behavioural difficulty, and that in the learning and reading difficulty categories gender differences were greater in the white group than in the black group. Male and female black pupils are more likely to be allocated to the 'learning difficulty' than to the 'reading difficulty' category compared with white pupils.

- Gender values may account for some of the discrepancies in special needs provision and school exclusions; but such values also appear to be affected by the impact of ethnicity and social class.

More research on special needs is needed to see how far teachers' assumptions about black and white masculinity and femininity account for these gender differences. Meanwhile, continuing concern about teachers' gender values and the loss (or lack) of in-service provision for practising teachers[21] has thrown the spotlight on initial teacher education, particularly in the UK, but also in European countries.[22] Student teachers in the United Kingdom receive some training in special needs, but very few report that they are encouraged to be pro-active in challenging gender inequalities in schools or to tackle sexism or sexual harassment.

[1]   Halpern (1992), p.170.

[2]   See Huston (1985); Archer & Lloyd (1985); Golombok & Fivush (1994) for reviews of research in this area.

[3]   See Huston (1985); Lloyd and Duveen (1992).

[4]   Maccoby and Jacklin (1974); Wylie (1979).

[5]   Renshaw (1990)

[6]   Dweck (1986); Dweck *et al* (1978).

[7]   Stables and Stables (1995).

[8]   See Hansford and Hattie (1982).

[9]   Davies (1989, 1993).

[10] Walkerdine (1990); Lloyd and Duveen (1992); Clark (1979).

[11] Harris, Nixon and Rudduck (1993).

[12] See also Chaplain, Miles and Rudduck(1994); Chaplain (1996).

[13] Williams *et al* (1996).

[14] Williams, *et al* (1996); Pitts and Smith (1995); MacLeod and Morris (1996); Balding *et al* (1996).

[15] Whitney and Smith (1993, p.8).

[16] Parsons (1995), para 4.5.

[17] Ford *et al* (1982).

[18] Cooper *et al* (1991); Riddell *et al* (1994); Riddell (1996).

[19] The study was conducted in 21 schools in one LEA that had a history of promoting equal opportunities and which also maintained a proportion of statements for SEN that was close to the national mean. One junior school had equal numbers of boys abd girls; another had eight times more boys than girls.

[20] 'Black' in this LEA refers to African–Caribbean and 'black other'; the category 'white' comprises 'white English' and 'white Irish'. Children who are learning English as a second language have been omitted from these data.

[21] See Arnot, David and Weiner (1996).

[22] Menter (1989); Skelton (1989); Coffey and Acker (1991); Crozier and Menter (1993); Poole and Isaacs (1993).

6 TRANSITIONS BETWEEN SCHOOL, WORK AND FAMILY LIFE

This chapter draws attention to research on the role played by social influences outside the school in shaping young people's response to schooling and their academic achievement. It focuses on the following questions:

To what extent have 'signals' from the labour market affected the motivation and behaviour of boys and girls, especially in relation to course choices and to decisions about staying on in education after 16?

What other social factors impinge on male and female patterns of educational achievement? What else influences young people's responses to education and their understanding of what it means to 'succeed'?

Although often speculative, small-scale studies of youth suggest the range of factors which schools might wish to consider in relation to gender performance. National surveys and local studies of ethnicity and social class also suggest that gender differences are not the same in different cultural groupings and that differences between boys or between girls could be more significant than those between the sexes.

6.1 'SIGNALS' FROM THE LABOUR MARKET

The argument in this section is that what goes on in the labour market affects how young people respond to educational opportunities.

Despite greater employment opportunities for women and more positive societal attitudes towards women working, the experiences of the two sexes are still rather different. Employment opportunities are still heavily structured by gender. For example, in the mid-1990s:

- 94% of men were economically active compared with around 72% of women. More women in their late rather than early twenties worked part-time reflecting the continued high child-care responsibilities of young women.

- men and women mainly worked in different occupational sectors. Women working full-time were 'heavily concentrated' in clerical and secretarial occupations (around 40% of 20-year-olds) and, to a lesser extent, in personal and service occupations (EOC, 1995, p.13). By contrast, men were more likely to be found in craft and related occupations and in plant and machine operative jobs. Many young women worked part-time as sales or check-out assistants in the retail trades and much of this work was associated with 'low skilled, low status and low paid occupations'.

Whilst there are major differences in employment opportunities for men and women, there is also evidence of some improvements. For example, roughly a quarter of men now work full-time in managerial, professional and associated professional occupations but recently the proportion of women in these sorts of occupations has begun to reach similar levels. However, whether the jobs they are actually doing are entirely comparable remains an open question. Many argue that a 'glass ceiling' still operates, especially at the highest levels.

- Occupational opportunities remain heavily structured by gender.
- When young men and women try to anticipate their futures after full-time education, they still receive different 'signals' from the labour market about male and female work opportunities.

During the course of the last decade the youth labour market has undergone substantial structural change. Traditional assumptions about what young people should do at 16 have been challenged by the rapid collapse of employment opportunities for 16-year-olds since the mid-1980s and by changing perceptions of the adequacy of the labour supply of highly-trained workers. Both developments have, in the short term, affected boys more than girls.

After leaving school at the minimum school-leaving age boys have traditionally entered apprenticeships in craft occupations. 'Early' leaving was encouraged. Entry to employment for young women, on the other hand, has usually been through a short period of participation in some form of post-16 training; secretarial jobs, for example, have typically demanded one year of further study in further education (Payne, 1995). In recent years, however, traditional routes into, for example, manufacturing industries, have collapsed. Many boys have as a result been forced to rethink their assumptions about staying on in full-time education.

At the same time views about the nature and importance of youth training have undergone considerable revision. In the mid-to-late-1980s new initiatives were launched to encourage young men and women to seek different kinds of training. In addition, changes in social security and benefit arrangements for 16- and 17-year-olds have contributed to the view that leaving school at the first opportunity was to be 'discouraged' (Raffe and Willms, 1989; but also Gray *et al*, 1992).

- Given the extent to which young men had dominated the take-up of apprenticeships and other forms of on-the-job training, they were disproportionately affected by the collapse of the youth labour market during the late eighties.

There are other signs that the employment future may look fairly bleak for certain groups of young men. Indeed, some economic commentators are predicting that as many as 70% of the new jobs which will be created in the United Kingdom over the next decade will be in areas traditionally dominated by women; the main areas of growth will be in managerial and other associated professional and clerical occupations (Hughes, 1996). Such 'signals' undoubtedly filter back into the school system and affect the climate of opportunity.

All social groups seem to have developed higher expectations in relation to participation in post-compulsory education. A number of factors seem to have been at work here. Crucially, a higher proportion of parents has been educated to higher post-compulsory levels and the proportion of the population in social classes I and II has expanded. These educationally and socially advantaged groups have, in turn, sought further opportunities for their offspring (Burnhill *et al*, 1990).

Choice of Post-16 Qualifications

Chapter 1 demonstrated the extent to which choices of A-level subjects have reflected traditional gender biases in relation to the Science–Arts divide. Although the proportion of women in further and higher education with science, engineering and technology backgrounds has increased, nevertheless most of the additional HE places in these subjects (35,000 between 1988 and 1991) have been taken up by men.[1] The differential in absolute numbers of men and women entering higher education courses to read science, engineering or technology has become greater every year.

Similarly the level of vocational course chosen is heavily shaped by traditional gender assumptions about men's and women's work. Women still tend to choose nursing, teaching and courses leading to high-level RSA qualifications; men continue to opt for HNDs/HNCs, BTEC highers, ONDs/ONCs, BTEC Nationals, and City & Guilds advanced craft certificates. Felstead and colleagues (1995) report that the greatest gender gaps in terms of levels of higher qualifications were in traditional male occupational areas; craft and related occupations, for example, had a 30% gap in favour of men. Indeed, even in female-dominated sectors (clerical, services and sales) more men than women held higher level vocational qualifications. Women have been acquiring qualifications in hitherto 'male-dominated' occupations, and gender biases in the new qualifications are becoming less pronounced, but these changes have still been modest (see also Bailey, 1992).

- Gender biases are being sustained in young men's and women's choices of vocational courses. Young women are still selecting business and commerce, hairdressing, and beauty and caring services, while young men are still choosing engineering, construction and mainstream science subjects.

Whether such traditional course choices after compulsory education are the cause or the symptom of sex segregation in the labour market is still a matter of contention. A major longitudinal study of the career preferences of 11- to 17-year-old pupils was conducted by the GIST project[2] in the early 1980s. Kelly's (1989) report on the survey data showed that even by the age of 11 there were 'enormous differences' between the sexes in relation to their job plans. Only 21% of girls and 11% of boys aged 11 said they would choose the same 'ideal' job; by the ages of 14 and 17, the overlaps were even smaller (12% and 8% respectively). Sex differentiation of job content affected all social groupings. Kelly concluded that 'the differences between girls' and boys' occupational plans were so large and consistent that it was meaningless to analyse the two sexes together' (p.189).

Although it is not yet clear what the impact of the National Curriculum is upon career preferences, recent research points to the positive attitudes of both boys and girls to physical sciences and technology during their teens, the relatively small differences in male and female performance in these subjects, and the increase in the number of women in science-related professions. Lightbody's and Durndell's (1996) work suggests that one of the reasons why these changes have not been translated into career choices may lie in the ways pupils translate their self-concepts into occupational decisions. Deep-seated views about what makes for a 'successful working life' still divide along gender-related lines.

6.2 SOCIAL FACTORS AFFECTING MALE AND FEMALE PATTERNS OF ACHIEVEMENT

Gender is not the only 'background factor' influencing pupils' levels of educational performance. Social class and ethnicity also have powerful effects. Figure 6.1 uses data from the Youth Cohort Study to show differences in examination results between boys and girls, between pupils from 'professional' backgrounds and 'manual' ones, and between whites, Asians (including Bangladeshi, Indian and Pakistani pupils) and African–Caribbeans (Drew and Gray, 1990).

The data presented in Figure 6.1 relate to a period a decade ago. Unfortunately, it has not proved possible to identify a more contemporary source of data on young people which simultaneously combines information on social class, ethnicity and gender. There are few signs that things have changed in the meantime. As the National Commission on Education (1993) put it:

> 'Children from social classes I and II do better, on average, in examinations at 16, are more likely to stay on longer in full-time education and are more likely to go to university than those in social classes III to V. *There has been little change over the years in the proportion of entrants to higher education who come from working class families*' (p.8, our emphasis).

It is important, of course, to remember that what is being referred to here are the *average* differences between the social classes; many pupils from working-class backgrounds do extremely well in terms of educational performance and, conversely, some middle-class pupils do rather badly. The extent to which the educational performances of the different social classes overlap suggest it would be unwise to adopt too 'deterministic' a view of educational life-chances associated with membership of particular social groups. On the other hand it would be naive to maintain that family background does not matter.

Figure 6.1

Average examination scores by social class background, ethnic origin and gender (1985)

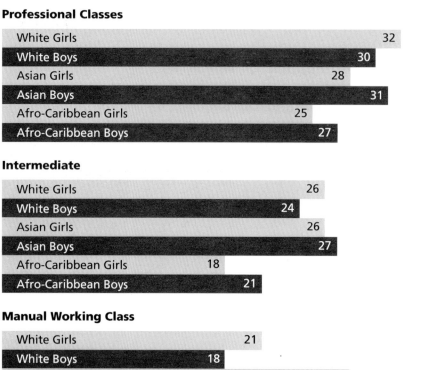

Professional Classes

White Girls	32
White Boys	30
Asian Girls	28
Asian Boys	31
Afro-Caribbean Girls	25
Afro-Caribbean Boys	27

Intermediate

White Girls	26
White Boys	24
Asian Girls	26
Asian Boys	27
Afro-Caribbean Girls	18
Afro-Caribbean Boys	21

Manual Working Class

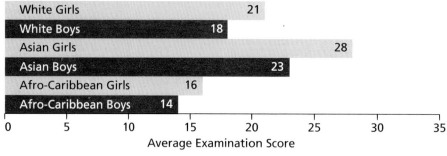

White Girls	21
White Boys	18
Asian Girls	28
Asian Boys	23
Afro-Caribbean Girls	16
Afro-Caribbean Boys	14

Average Examination Score

Source: Youth Cohort Study, Drew and Gray, 1990, adapted from p.114, Table 5.

Figure 6.1 suggests that there were some clear differences between boys and girls within each of the three social class groups. White girls from professional backgrounds did better on average than white boys from similar backgrounds; the same was also true for the intermediate and working-class groups. Particular attention should perhaps be drawn to the position of white working-class males. The numerical size of this group and their relatively low levels of average performance have made them a very 'visible' group within many schools.

Figure 6.1 also touches on differences in performance between ethnic groups but here rather more up-to-date information is available. Much of it has recently been summarised by Gillborn and Gipps (1996), using data from English local authorities with some of the largest ethnic minority populations.[3] Figure 6.2 shows the position in Birmingham (a very large LEA) between 1992 and 1995.[4]

The general trends in Figure 6.2 are already familiar. In whichever year one compares the performance of white girls in Birmingham with white boys, the girls are always doing better and usually by a quite noticeable margin. The same observation is true for African–Caribbean girls in comparison with African–Caribbean boys, although in some years the gap is a good deal smaller. In terms of absolute performance levels, one should not ignore, however, the extent to which African–Caribbean girls *and* boys were lagging behind white boys and all three groups were some distance behind white girls.

Figure 6.2

15–16-year-olds gaining five or more GCSE higher grade passes, by ethnicity and gender (Birmingham 1992–1995)

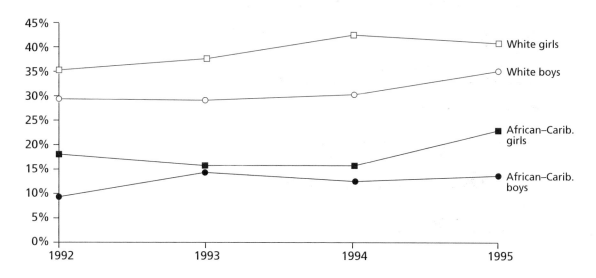

Figure 6.1 suggests that Asian boys and girls both do well in relation to their white counterparts. The weakness of these data, of course, is that pupils from very different 'Asian' backgrounds are grouped together into one category. Recent data from Birmingham LEA suggest that boys and girls of Asian origin perform at around the same levels and that gender differences are less significant than ethnic differences, especially in relation to lower-achieving pupils. Boys and girls of Bangladeshi background, for example, are the most likely of all ethnic groups to leave without *any* educational qualifications whatsoever; pupils from Indian backgrounds are the least likely to leave without any qualifications; whilst pupils from Pakistani backgrounds fall somewhere in between (Gillborn, 1997, p.13).

One other feature of the educational experiences of these various ethnic groups also suggests that simple generalisations are difficult to sustain. Pupils from nearly all ethnic minorities have, in recent years, been considerably more likely than their white counterparts to participate in post-compulsory education (Drew *et al*, 1997; National Commission on Education, 1993) – although the reasons why are not entirely clear (Drew *et al*, 1992).

Finally, the effects of locality need to be considered, albeit briefly. Whilst some generalisations about the performance of different social and ethnic groups are possible at the *national* level, the often complex social and ethnic make-up of different localities often makes it quite difficult even for neighbouring schools to compare themselves meaningfully with national patterns.

- Gender is one of the key factors affecting educational performance but it always functions in relation to other social variables such as social class, ethnic origin and local context which also exercise powerful and independent effects.

- The extent to which one or other ethnic or social class group and one gender dominates the lowest achieving group depends on the local context.

6.3 CONCEPTS OF SUCCESS: THE INFLUENCE OF CONTEMPORARY YOUTH CULTURES

In recent years researchers focusing on disaffected youth have moved substantially away from individualised explanations for 'poor' performance such as deficit models of low self-esteem, poor family support or reduced motivation. Instead, they have turned their attention to how particular versions of masculinity and femininity are constructed by pupils in relation both to school cultures and societal influences. Peer groups reflect prevailing versions of masculinity and femininity and these, in turn, come to define what 'success' is to mean at school, especially for pupils of secondary age.

There have been a number of studies of peer group cultures in secondary schools, particularly of boys' friendship groups in the lowest academic streams (e.g. Hargreaves, 1967; Willis, 1977; Jenkins, 1983; Brown, 1987; Gillborn, 1990). Such studies suggest that the ways in which pupils are organised (whether in streams, bands or sets) can have considerable impact on how pupils perceive themselves, especially if some are labelled 'successful', and others 'failures'. According to some researchers, peer group cultures are an *indirect result* of such curriculum strategies. Thus anti-school attitudes amongst pupils may be reinforced by the school even if strategies such as streaming do not cause them (Ball, 1981; Berends, 1995). More recent case studies of comprehensive schools have suggested that a greater emphasis on school performance and competition for pupils is affecting how teachers respond to pupils and contributing to the creation of a new range of pupil sub-cultures (e.g. Mac an Ghaill, 1994; Sewell, 1997).

> • Peer group cultures play a central role in determining what young people come to define as 'success' at school. Schools in turn may be involved in the formation of such cultures to a greater extent than is often recognised.

Case studies of particular schools or groups of youths since the late 1970s have provided powerful insights into the processes which contribute to the development of peer group cultures, especially forms of resistance to schooling and the ways young people 'come to terms' in their own way with their expected destinations in the labour market. There is no suggestion, of course, that such outcomes are inevitable; unfortunately, far less work has been undertaken by researchers in this field into those circumstances where disaffected peer groups might be expected to emerge but, in practice, do not. There are also other difficulties in generalising too readily from research. Whilst such studies may provide an adequate account of why some male groups have stood still in educational terms, they provide little by way of insight into the improvements in performance other groups (and notably girls) have achieved over the last decade (Furlong, 1986). With the virtual collapse of traditional modes of entry into employment for young men and, to a lesser extent, young women, so-called 'cultures of resistance' have taken on new and different forms.

To understand the diversity of achievement patterns three important transitions to adulthood need to be considered. These are the transition into: (a) the labour market (getting a job); (b) the marriage market (getting a husband/wife); and (c) the sexual market (being sexually attractive) (Wallace, 1987).

Changing Girls, Changing Times?

Major shifts in girls' attitudes to their future lives are now being identified by researchers. At this stage we can only speculate about how prevalent they are and whether they may account for the improvement in girls' educational performance. What then would account for the continuation of traditionally female course choices after 16?

Various studies[5] suggest that young women's aspirations are conditioned by a series of *pragmatic* choices. They have a realistic understanding of the difficulties facing women in the labour market and as working parents. But, at the same time, there are signs that major shifts are taking place in how girls value work and family life.

Economic Independence

Young women today are reported as accepting many of the principles of equal opportunities, especially insofar as they endorse women's rights to economic independence and personal respect.[6] There is evidence that working-class girls, for example, do not wish to follow in their mothers' footsteps (in terms of type of female office/factory work)[7] and are being encouraged by their mothers[8] or their fathers not to do so.[9] Career planning is also being encouraged amongst some groups of girls, especially since increased opportunities are available in the professions (Roker, 1993). Studies of middle-class girls' achievement suggest that parents and schools assume that they will have 'unfettered careers' which incorporate periods of child-rearing (McLaren, 1996; Kenway, 1995).

Early career planning has been reported as a cause of stress to some high-achieving girls (Lucey and Walkerdine, 1996); it also delays rather than resolves the conflict between family and work. Nonetheless, as Bates and Riseborough (1993) point out, such planning may be providing the possibility for non-traditional choices to be made by those girls who are the most qualified and who have the strongest material advantages.

The quest for individual autonomy and upward social mobility that Mirza (1992) found amongst 'achieving' African–Caribbean girls are now reported to be shared by white working-class girls (Sharpe, 1992; Lees, 1993) and by Asian Muslim girls (Basit, 1996). An extensive survey of the 18–34-year-old generation of young women[10] also indicated that young women were now more likely to support such values as independence, risk, hedonism and 'living on the edge', and to 'be committed to achieving success'.

- There are some indications of a 'sea-change' in female attitudes towards career planning, family and work. However, there is still evidence of considerable variation between different groups of girls.

Personal Relationships

A number of studies suggests that girls' attitudes towards educational success may be changing because of their different aspirations with regard to personal relationships and adult life. The evidence, although not conclusive, suggests that girls today are reluctant to adopt the label of being a 'feminist' (Wilkinson, 1994; Sharpe, 1994), but at the same time they are incorporating some of the principles of feminism into their personal lives.[11] For example, young women in their quest for autonomy may be giving active consideration to new models of family life – equal parenting, contingency planning[12] or role reversal. Sharpe's follow-up study of schoolgirls found that marriage appeared less attractive in 1992 than in 1976. At the moment it is not clear how fast these tendencies are developing or whether they seriously challenge the traditional assumption that female achievement means 'getting a man', rather than a career (McRobbie, 1978).

- More research is needed to discover whether girls' increased valuing of independence is encouraging them to improve their academic performance.

Tensions Between Family and Work

Such changing values come into conflict with girls' awareness of sex segregation and sex discrimination in the labour market and the lack of female economic power (Sharpe, 1992, Gaskell, 1992). The pressures on girls to resolve the family–work conflict by opting for security and by 'preferring not to resist the inevitable' remain powerful (Gaskell, 1992). Consequently, they continue to choose traditionally feminine training routes and occupations, still wanting 'people jobs', avoiding work contexts that might cause stress (such as being in a minority) and valuing female friendships at work (Sharpe, 1994).

Other circumstances also affect how far girls are likely to succeed. New research by Adkins and Leonard (1996) is considering the extent to which domestic work is likely to act as a major constraint on *working-class girls'* academic achievement both before and after the school-leaving age. They are far more likely than boys (or middle-class girls) to be involved in domestic, caring and emotional work in the home, including care of younger siblings or their own offspring. But domestic work also requires a set of skills and provides relevant experience for some of the toughest forms of female employment - what Skeggs (1988) calls 'domestic apprenticeships'. Indeed, candidates for so-called 'feminine' training courses may be screened for such feminine skills[13] (Bates and Riseborough, 1993).

- Lower levels of educational performance and traditionally feminine course choices amongst certain groups of girls may be linked to their domestic circumstances, their awareness of the continuing patterns of sex-segregation in local labour markets and the lack of adequate childcare.

Changing Boys, Changing Times?

That boys have been falling behind in recent years in terms of educational achievement is undeniable. Researchers of peer-group cultures suggested that boys' educational performance is linked to their concepts of *masculinity* and masculine definitions of what it means to succeed and fail.

Masculine Identities

There appears to be a range of adolescent masculine identities. These have been shaped partly in response to ethnic and social origins and social contexts, and partly in response to school experiences. The variety of masculine identities amongst male pupils in any one school is likely, of course, to differ. Brown (1987) has identified three different 'frames of reference' used by working-class boys: those who wanted to 'get out', those who wanted to 'get on', and the lads who wanted to 'stay in' working-class communities. Today it is common to refer to such frames of reference as representing different '*masculinities*'.[14]

During the 1980s, the transition to adulthood required a new set of responses from those 'ordinary kids' who had previously assumed they would take up traditional apprenticeships. Staying on in education after 16, in what some regarded as 'suspended animation', was one such response (Willis, 1985). However, some working-class boys are reported to be adapting to the new vocational/modernising influences and curricular subjects (such as technology and computer studies) and are seeking new occupations that might not only protect them from the insecurities of the labour market but also secure them higher wages. One researcher (Mac an Ghaill, 1994) has described this group as the 'new enterprisers'.

The Macho Lads

A second theme is that economic change has encouraged rather than discouraged the continued presence of a group of disaffected 'macho lads'. This group is becoming increasingly separated from the mainstream with its emphasis on the importance of achieving credentials. Studies of working-class communities in Belfast and South Wales reported the continued presence of Willis's 'lads' (1977) with their particular forms of confrontational style and their aspirations to become 'real men' (Jenkins, 1983; Brown, 1987). At a time of relatively full employment, the 'lads' celebrated the tough physical manual labour of their fathers and the 'macho culture' in which men were the main wage earners, the future breadwinners and heads of households, as well as 'dominant males'. Rather than perceiving themselves as failures, the lads celebrated the early transition into employment as a means of achieving full manhood.

Connell's (1989) study of a group of unemployed working-class men in Australia shows how unemployment had affected their lives. They felt that they had been denied access to traditional male forms of power at school (such as higher education, elite occupations and higher wages). They responded by becoming the 'cool guys', taking pride in courting trouble, challenging the authority of the school and claiming other sources of power - such as *sporting prowess, physical aggression and sexual conquest*. These forms of 'gender power' became their new symbols of class identity and the basis of a new contest over the dominant forms of 'masculinity'.

Mac an Ghaill's (1994) study of a school in the Midlands develops Connell's themes. Facing the loss of traditional male employment and finding themselves in a competitive school culture, some valued new models of a 'business-like' masculinity. In contrast the macho-lads responded to their academic failure and their negative employment prospects by celebrating the '3 F's' ('fighting, football and ****ing'). In short, they coped with the multiple uncertainties of their positions by promoting a *'hyper-masculinity'*. Similarly, Sewell's controversial study of African–Caribbean boys in one school suggests that those who are 'the rebels' celebrate a hyper-sexual version of masculinity – what he calls 'phallocentric masculinity'. In both studies, boys' concepts of masculinity allow them to regain control of the situations they find themselves in, but can also result in conflict with the school.

Family and Work

The ways in which boys relate to femininity and to the family is a third theme in recent studies. Research suggests that, although there have been some changes in boys' attitudes towards women's roles in the work sphere and some acceptance of the principle of equal opportunities,[15] the majority of boys are still reluctant to consider a sharing of domestic responsibilities and especially childcare/parenting roles. This may be associated with the devaluing of particular school subjects and occupations which are seen as too 'feminine' (e.g. teaching young children, nursing).

Evidence on what boys now value in relation to fatherhood, marriage and domesticity is sparse (Wallace, 1987), although Lees (1998) recently found that boys were more likely than girls to retain traditional notions of the male-headed family with mothers at home caring for the children. Such aspirations, whilst encouraging some to gain qualifications, may, however, be based on the need to retain a traditional role outside the work sphere in the context of economic uncertainty.

Research on the masculine identities of youth demonstrate how they are shaped in opposition to concepts of femininity and around particular notions of what it is to be a heterosexual male (Mac an Ghaill, 1994). For those boys lucky enough to be on the inside of a friendship group, support for particular versions of masculinity is found in male bonding (*homosociality*). But boys may attempt to define heterosexual masculinity by putting down girls (*misogyny*) or by allegations of homosexuality against other boys (Holland *et al*, 1993). *Homophobia* can be a major source of tension in some schools and can be the focus of bullying. Such strategies serve a purpose; they allow boys to 'police' acceptable versions of masculinity.

The aspirations of girls and boys in relation to adult life do not necessarily develop at the same time. Girls' changing aspirations in relation to work, family and personal life may well impinge on boys' expectations, in some cases encouraging a greater flexibility in relation to male roles in society, in other cases reinforcing traditional or even 'hyper' notions of masculinity. The consequences of such concepts of masculinity are only now being explored. A key question being addressed is whether boys' failure to take sufficient account of current changes in family life and work conditions affects their academic performance. Does the lack of flexibility in relation to gender roles have implications for boys' motivation to learn and to adapt to changing economic climates where job opportunities might be on offer, but which cannot be taken up for fear of reducing their sense of manhood?

Much of this is new territory for schools in the United Kingdom. The nature and extent of the influences at play in relation to masculinity is recognised, but strategic thinking about how to intervene is still at an early stage.[16] Experiences in some Australian schools need to be borne in mind; Kenway (1996), for example, reports that some equal opportunities interventions had produced 'overly negative responses' in boys. To get round this Salisbury and Jackson (1996) suggest some new ways in which teachers might work directly with boys on issues of masculinity.

- Peer group cultures and their definitions of masculinity and femininity play an important role in disaffection and underachievement; more research is needed on schools' capacities to challenge or reduce the impact of certain negative images of masculinity and femininity on pupils' performance and subject choices.

---

[1]   Committee on Women in Science, Engineering and Technology, 1994, p14.

[2]   The sample was drawn from ten co-educational comprehensive schools.

[3]   The London Boroughs of Brent and Lambeth, and Birmingham LEA.

[4] Thanks are due to David Gillborn for providing us with this graph based on data from the Birmingham Education Department.

[5] Gaskell (1992); Skeggs(1988); Sharpe (1994).

[6] Wilkinson (1994); Wilkinson and Mulgan (1995).

[7] Sharpe (1994).

[8] Mann (1997) reported that successful working-class, female A-level students in her sample were being encouraged by those mothers who had already made the 'transition' to greater autonomy for themselves either through work, their marriages or relations with men, or through more education. Mirza (1992) found that Afro-Caribbean mothers did not press their daughters to repeat their mistakes; Basit's (1996) sample of Asian Muslim girls positively distanced themselves from their mothers' work but also were encouraged to aim higher by their parents.

[9] Lucey and Walkerdine (1996) report finding that some 'successful' working-class girls are being strongly encouraged by their fathers.

[10] Wilkinson (1994); Wilkinson and Mulgan (1995)

[11] Griffin (1989); Condor (1989); Blackmore *et al* (1996); Frazer (1989).

[12] Contingency planning is where each partner takes turns to plan the two careers in tandem.

[13] Bates's (1993) study of caring for the aged courses and fashion & design illustrates how this works in practice; see also Gaskell's (1992) study of clerical courses in Canada. One could argue that the same sort of 'domestication' process occurs with primary teaching, making it harder for men to demonstrate appropriate qualities.

[14] Connell (1995); Mac an Ghaill (1994, 1996).

[15] Oakley (1996); Wilkinson and Mulgan (1995).

[16] For example, the EC-funded Project Arianne is using four pilot secondary schools in England and in eight other European countries. The project is focused on developing strategies for teachers to work more effectively with boys and is co-ordinated by Madeleine Arnot; Bray *et al* (1997) also offers strategies for improving boys' performance.

PART 4

THE AGENDA IN SCHOOLS

7 SCHOOL STRATEGIES AND POLICIES

7.1 THE CHANGING AGENDA

This section looks at work on gender carried out in and by schools over the last 20 years. Schools have been the site of considerable small-scale research and development activity, much of it initiated by teachers themselves. Several different 'phases' of national concern can be identified in which different kinds of enquiry and intervention were promoted. The *equal opportunities phase* was marked by concern mainly about girls' experiences within male-dominated structures – in society in general and in relation to school knowledge and organisation in particular. Activity in schools focused on reviewing and seeking to change the gendered images of subjects and patterns of options' choices, the presentation of knowledge in curriculum texts, aspects of school organisation and patterns of classroom interaction.[1]

In time, the equal opportunities concerns gave way to concerns expressed more in terms of *equity* and *social justice* – terms which 'heralded an approach...which would embrace concerns about boys and girls, and would seek to understand how race, poverty and ethnicity complicate the picture of gendered outcomes' (Martinez, 1994, p.5). Progress was still largely dependent on the concern and commitment of individual heads, individual and small groups of teachers, and the active support of the equal opportunities advisers that some LEAs appointed to raise the profile of gender work in schools.

The *Technical and Vocational Education Initiative* (TVEI) could be said to constitute a phase in its own right in that it was the first major initiative, backed by a powerful government agency (the Training Agency), to promote an 'explicit commitment' to equity issues (Bridgwood, 1989, p.1). It sought to achieve its ends through curriculum re-organisation and was particularly concerned to encourage more girls to take up technology. A central tenet was that 'girls and boys should normally be taught together and care should be taken to avoid discrimination and sex stereotyping'.

It offered schools financial incentives to develop work in line with TVEI values, and the Training Agency had 'the authority to withhold funding if TVEI criteria were not met' (Millman and Weiner, 1987, p.167). It foreshadowed the national curriculum in moving from options (which often resulted in gendered subject choices) to 'providing substantial compulsory elements' in the TVEI curriculum (*ibid*, p.173). It brought equal opportunity issues sharply into focus, encouraged the development of whole-school approaches and endorsed the professional responsibility of schools to base their interventions on analyses of their own performance data, thus anticipating the *achievement-oriented phase* that is now prevalent.

7.2 SCHOOL STRATEGIES

This section focuses on strategies that were prominent within and across the different phases of work on gender issues: *single-sex grouping* and *role modelling*, developed in the 'equal opportunities' phase and now at the centre of a rather different debate; *whole-school policy development*, a strategy that grew out of the TVEI phase and that continues, in a slightly different form, in the 'achievement-oriented phase'; and *mentoring strategies* which are a recent addition to the portfolio of school-based gender initiatives.

Single-sex Groupings

Single-sex groupings in curriculum subjects: some examples

The idea of arranging single-sex groupings in co-educational schools was in part a response to analyses of data on classroom interaction and options choices which showed girls at a disadvantage. Single-sex groupings (Kruse, 1992, p.81) provided opportunities for them to enhance their competence in particular subjects (mainly science and mathematics) – but also for boys to strengthen their engagement and performance in subjects that were traditionally seen as 'for girls' – such as modern languages and English.

Researchers urge caution in interpreting and acting on the findings of evaluation studies in this area given the difficulty of controlling the variables and the often narrow and short-term focus. Harvey looked at single-sex groupings in science in the first year of secondary schooling, comparing the test performances of pupils in single-sex groups in two mixed schools, six girls' schools and three boys' schools, and in mixed groups in six mixed schools. He concluded that 'single-sex groups in science, whether in mixed schools or in single-sex schools, do not improve the attainment of girls in first-year science' (1985, p.179). In a later paper (with Stables, 1986) he suggests that single-sex groupings might, however, help to change stereotyped gendered *attitudes* to subjects. In reviewing relevant research the authors are properly cautious, arguing the small number of studies and the difficulty of generalisation. Smith's study showed that in one secondary school girls taught for the first two years in a single-sex group for mathematics managed to sustain their achievements relative to girls who had the same average marks on the same test at the beginning of the two years but who were taught in a mixed group (1984, pp.77–81); and Powell's 1979 study, also in one school, showed gains in achievement for boys when learning modern languages in single-sex groups. Rennie and Parker (1987), building on these earlier studies, set up an experiment in science in which they controlled the teacher variable but at the cost of having single-sex groupings consisting of only two or three pupils per group. They concluded that mixed-sex groups can be effective if 'hands-on' experience is equally accessible to both girls and boys (p.72). Perhaps the most important contribution of this group of studies is to remind us of the ways in which pupils' experiences vary from context to context – and in particular from teacher to teacher – and that generalisation is therefore very difficult.

In Australia there was concern that 'the establishment of single-sex classes in co-educational schools seemed to be growing faster than the substantive evidence to justify it' (Rowe, 1988, p.180). A sustained study of girls' learning in mathematics was therefore mounted in one Australian post-primary school where Y7 and Y8 girls and boys were randomly placed in single-sex ('treatment') classes and mixed-sex ('control') classes; their performance was studied over time. For all other subjects pupils were taught in mixed-sex classes. The early findings (and there are several caveats about the design) suggest a link between single-sex classes and growth in confidence in the subject which in turn may affect achievement. Rowe comments: 'The long-term effectiveness of single-sex class grouping as an appropriate intervention strategy .... (for any area of the curriculum) has yet to be established' (p.197) and that 'additional data need to be gathered before an informed, responsible judgement advocating the universal efficacy of establishing single-sex classes in co-educational post-primary schools could be made' (p.198).

Where these studies have been mostly concerned with attitude to the subject and self-confidence, other more process-oriented studies have looked at pupils' *responses* to being organised in single-sex groupings. The data suggest that girls respond more positively to the new situation than do boys. According to Kenway, boys in a single-sex mathematics class in Australia 'mounted a litany of complaints because without the girls .... they had no-one to help them or compete with and no-one to keep their behaviour under control' (1995, p.68) – a restatement of the familiar 'gentling' or 'service' role performed by female pupils in mixed groups. According to Crump (1990, p.371, discussing research by Bowes) boys put into single-sex science groups showed a 'lingering resentment and lesser ability to cope with the change' whereas girls were more ready to take advantage of the opportunity. Measor *et al* (1996) observed six schools where single-sex groupings of 14- to 15-year-olds were set up for sex education. They reported that girls liked the girls-only grouping and were serious and closely engaged, whereas boys disrupted the lesson through mockery, laughter and competitive bragging. The researchers concluded that there is a need for 'innovative teaching strategies which reach boys more effectively' – but which also 'protect space for the girls' interests.'

Single-sex groupings across the curriculum

An HMI Inspection Report (1986) notes an interesting development in a secondary school. Single-sex grouping was introduced across the curriculum in years 7 and 8 and was sustained through to year 11 in mathematics, English, PE and religious and personal development; mixed-sex teaching was introduced in about 60% of subjects in the third year (now year 9). The report (written when the scheme was new) commented on the potential advantages – less polarised options choices, more dialogue among girls in mathematics classes and a more positive response among boys to English – and the possible disadvantage that views might become 'sharply polarised .... because boys and girls are not examining together their different perspectives sufficiently often'. The report of a full inspection (published eight years later) noted that the initiative in single-sex grouping was still in place. It was very positive about the school's work generally but acknowledged that because of major national changes to the curriculum during the intervening period it was difficult to estimate the contribution of the single-sex groupings to the overall pattern of performance. More information is needed on the longer-term effects of such initiatives.

A new focus for single-sex groupings

Some teachers and researchers argue that long-term progress on gender and achievement means helping pupils to discuss and challenge, initially in single-sex groupings, the social construction of gendered behaviour. The approach acknowledges that 'both boys and girls are limited by concepts of masculinity and femininity which narrow their options and experiences' (Martinez, 1994, p.9) and it seeks to provide 'space and possibilities' to help young people to think differently, act differently, 'and thus create change' (Kruse, 1992, pp.91–92). The approach recognises that young people will need support – from peers as well as from teachers – in exploring and trying out alternatives given that a common way for boys to demonstrate 'their credentials as male' is to 'patrol infringements of masculinity on the part of other boys' (Martinez, 1994, p.7). The message is that schools can, through pedagogic strategies, help loosen the dominance of gendered behaviour (see also Chapter 6).

Diane Reay (1990) describes her use of single-sex groups in a primary school. The move was originally prompted by concern about girls' lack of assertiveness and low self-esteem, but increasingly she wanted to encourage the boys to work together without – as they had done in a mixed-sex group – expressing their 'masculine power' by finding a sub-group of potentially vulnerable boys to mock and disturb: in a single-sex context, she claims, teachers can support boys in questioning and analysing peer group hierarchies in a forum that is non-threatening and non-confrontational (p.281). Progress was judged, at least initially, in terms of a change of 'attitudes and feelings' among both girls and boys, but change of attitude could be seen as a precondition of improved performance.

From Denmark, Anne-Marie Kruse (1992) describes a similar approach – the 'polarisation pedagogy' – which helps young people to confront 'stereotyped gendered behaviour patterns' (1992, p.98). She argues in particular that 'Boys need the opportunity to explore and change their ambivalent views of women, to be confronted with the effects of the misuse of power' (p.83) and to explore 'what it means and *can* mean to be a man and what masculinity may be' (p.82). In this approach, pioneered with 11-year-old pupils, periods of single-sex grouping, where gendered identities are explicitly explored, alternate with mixed-sex teaching.

It is not easy, for a number of reasons, to assess the impact of single-sex groupings on achievement. The experimental period may be short (and it takes time before the potential benefits of single-sex groupings are discernible in academic performance), and/or other variables may obscure the neatness of the experimental situation. This is not to say that experimenting with single-sex grouping is not worth while in the particular circumstances of particular schools. Crump (1990) offers some realistic advice: first, that if single-sex groupings are to succeed, then broad 'altruistic goals', such as 'empowering' girls or boys, need to be recast and 'linked closely in a student's mind to those practical issues which students feel are important to their futures' (p.372). Rennie and Parker (1987) argue that single-sex groupings may be particularly 'beneficial .... where teachers have a low level of awareness and skills in relation to creating and maintaining' an effective learning environment in *mixed* classes (p.65).

Role Modelling

Role modelling strategies have brought people from the locality into schools (usually for a one-off event, such as Equal People Day) who challenge gendered employment stereotypes (for example, women working on construction sites as surveyors or buyers, male nursery nurses, female carpenters). Sometimes a one-to-one 'mentoring' relationship with a successful same-sex outsider is set up and sustained over a period of time.

Schools have also been aware of the potential of role modelling within the staff group itself and are more sensitive to the messages given by the gendered divisions of labour and power among middle and senior management teams[2] (see Davies, 1990, p.61). However, the debate is now focusing more on the messages embedded in routine classroom practice and in the gendered culture of the school. The concern about boys' performance is prompting questions, here and in other countries, about the 'feminisation' of learning in the early years of schooling and the relative absence of male role models, and whether, for instance, boys come to see reading and writing as 'women's work'[3] (see also Chapter 2).

Whole-school Policy Development

Patrick Orr (1985, p.21) reported that there were relatively few schools in the 1980s where work on gender was 'underpinned by a "whole-school policy"'. The situation is now very different. The move has been from individual initiatives by committed teachers and islands of informed action to coherent policy requirements operating across all areas of institutional practice.

Developing a whole-school policy is not easy. Published accounts suggest that progress is helped if senior staff support the initiative and if the staff as a whole are prepared to engage in a critical review of the school's (and their own) practices, exposing assumptions about gender that familiarity has made acceptable. 'What is most striking', said Acker (1988, p.310), 'is the unselfconscious way in which mixed schools have used sex as a convenient administrative divider to organise registers, seat allocation, queuing, even coat-hanging'. It means coming to terms with what Arnot (1982) refers to as the school's 'gender code' and Kessler *et al* (1987) the 'gender regime' – that is, the ways in which institutions routinely determine roles and communicate expectations that reflect a set of gendered images and assumptions (see also Chapter 5). It means orchestrating a coherent shift towards a new set of values and making sure that they are consistently applied.

Reviews of whole-school gender approaches highlight two issues: one concerns the problem of securing whole-staff support, in practice as well as in principle, for whole-school policies. The second concerns the maintenance of the practices endorsed by the policy over time. A series of school sketches (see Rudduck, 1994, pp.82–116) documents aspects of the first problem. In one school where the senior management team was leading the development of a whole-school policy, teachers' personal stances were fairly evenly fanned out between the extremes of 'adversary' and 'advocate'. The central challenge was to find a formulation of intent that such a diverse collection of colleagues could sincerely commit themselves to. This is not easy, as Blackmore *et al* (1996), generalising from experience in Australia, have pointed out:

'...the issue of gender was overtly threatening to many...because it required them to change not just their classroom practice but to critically assess their everyday private as well as their public social practices.' (p.273)

A related problem is the provenance of the policy itself. The authors suggest (p.275) that school gender policies may represent the values and discourse of an institutional elite, produced in private and then made public but not always widely negotiated, with serious consequences for the translation of the policy into collective institutional action that goes beyond surface compliance.

An alternative approach is for schools to avoid dysfunctional internal conflicts by presenting work on gender as a *professional* responsibility of the staff as a whole that leaves aside individual views on gender and equity. Such an approach takes *outcomes* as the starting point; teachers work back from an analysis of gendered patterns of achievement to look at factors in the school that are preventing them from meeting their obligation to ensure that all pupils are performing at the far edge of their capacity.

Another issue is how to sustain commitment over time. Evidence from countries which have a recent history of mandated policy in schools is of value here. The national evaluation (Imsen, 1996) of the outcomes of the gender equality policy in Norway (in place since 1974) suggests that gender work has come, over time, to have a low priority on the *school's* agenda for action (new national concerns have tended to displace it) but that the issues are being addressed fairly consistently by *individual* teachers as a regular dimension of their curriculum work.

Performance Data Analysis and Mentoring Strategies

By the mid-1990s the national preoccupation with achievement created a new wave of concern about gender issues which is directly performance-oriented. The mechanism at the secondary level is straightforward and compelling: schools depend for income on pupil numbers, parental choice of school is influenced by published reports of examination results and league tables, underachieving boys can lower a school's overall performance profile.

What is important about the current orientation is that schools are able to construct their own analysis of the situation, based on internal scrutiny of performance data, and are able to tailor action to context.[4] There are, however, some costs to this approach. First, a considerable resource (of time and energy) is being spent on the analysis of data. Second, achievement tends to be rather narrowly defined in terms of examination performance and interventions may therefore be geared to short-term goals – strategies may be favoured which yield 'immediate, highly visible solutions' rather than those that work over a longer time frame to deal with the sources of disadvantage that are deeply embedded in the culture of schools and society. Third, the strategy may result in teacher support being directed towards potentially higher-achieving pupils rather than towards lower-achieving pupils.

Current concerns have brought a new strategy into the portfolio of possible interventions by schools: this is the targeting of individual or small groups of pupils for support, a strategy often referred to as 'mentoring' (but not in the earlier sense of providing role models to emulate). Mentoring is usually about one-to-one support from a member of the senior management team or from a subject teacher – or, in some schools, from older pupils or outsiders. Sometimes mentors work with small groups of pupils.

In secondary schools those most likely to be targeted for mentoring are pupils in years 10 and 11 who are thought to be at risk of underachieving, but increasingly mentoring is being introduced with pupils deemed to be 'at risk' in the lower years of secondary schools and in primary schools.

Two recent studies show how rapidly the 'target and support' strategy has spread among secondary schools. Quicke (1995) collected data by questionnaire from 24 schools across two midlands LEAs, and Millman and Weiner (1987) collected data from 29 schools in the eastern region of the country. Quicke comments that the majority were concerned about boys' performance and were developing some form of mentoring support: in some, the mentoring was mainly for boys and in others for 'borderline' boys *and* girls. The eastern region study showed a similar readiness among secondary schools to adopt mentoring strategies to raise achievement. The repertoire of mentoring strategies is increasing and includes: a formal achievement panel to which boys at risk, and their parents, are summoned; linking sixth formers with underachieving younger pupils; and 'vacation classes' run by volunteer teachers for pupils who are falling behind.

Quicke's study identified some peripheral shortcomings of mentoring strategies: for instance, pupils might not feel comfortable with the mentor they have been assigned (1995, p.5). More significantly he found some evidence to suggest that in schools where examination results have improved 'with respect to the number of five A*–Cs, the results lower down have worsened' (p.7). It seems that there is now an achievement-oriented culture – but one that may be in danger of increasing the 'dividing practices' in schools.

A recent study of the school improvement strategies adopted by 'improving' schools suggests that mentoring has frequently been adopted to 'get things moving' (Wilcox *et al*, 1996). After a year or two, however, the demanding nature of this approach, in terms of teachers' time, and the pressure to involve more pupils (often coming from the pupils themselves) may dilute the impact. Reflecting on their experiences, several schools have seen it as an important but temporary stepping stone in their moves towards greater effectiveness.

7.3 COMMENTS

Some schools have considerable experience of work on gender and the current focus on performance is merely a new phase; for others, the high profile given to the issue nationally has been a catalyst, encouraging them to monitor progress in their own setting and to plan appropriate interventions. In some areas, LEAs offer a framework of support, setting up subject-oriented review groups, offering guidance on relevant resources, and undertaking and feeding back detailed statistical analyses of performance data within and across schools. Other agencies (for example, SCAA through its working party on boys and English, or the QUASE and YELLIS projects through their analyses of schools' year 11 examination data, are providing focused evidence and advice.

From the accounts of activities made available to the authors of this report, it is clear that teachers are committed to understanding the situation in their own school as a basis for action. This seems important given the extent of local variation in performance patterns. As one teacher said, we need to know what characterises a potential underachiever in *this* school and what helps pupils who are making good progress in *this* school to sustain their motivation.

In looking critically at structures, practices and relationships in their own schools, teachers have clearly had to confront many of the issues explored in earlier chapters of this report. The initiatives they have taken represent a (somewhat opportunist) mix of guidance from various sources. Studies of school and classroom initiatives undertaken by teachers and researchers in schools, as this chapter indicates, have tended to be small-scale and short-term, and to focus more on attitudes and process than outcomes. There is, therefore, little definitive evidence of the way that particular strategies are affecting pupils' performance over time. There is a need for more longitudinal studies.

What is clear, however, is that schools are concerned about the issue of gender and performance, are giving it serious attention, are working collaboratively with people from other schools, from local authority services and from higher education departments to develop appropriate strategies and policies, and are receptive to the guidance that research can offer. The issue of how research on gender is best collated, evaluated and disseminated so that it can influence thinking and practice in schools remains – but is one that reports such as this are attempting to address.

---

[1] For evidence see Arnot, David and Weiner, 1996.

[2] Edwards and Lyons (1996), citing 1993 figures, claim that of the 196,632 full-time teachers in secondary schools in England and Wales roughly half are men and half women but that 78% of heads are male. The authors acknowledge that the balance in favour of women has improved over the last three years and that in some areas (some inner London boroughs for instance) the percentage of female heads of mixed secondary schools is above the average. NUT figures for January 1994 report that with roughly half the teachers in secondary schools male and half female, 79.8% of heads are male and only 20.2% are female. Figures for primary schools where 82% of teachers are women indicate that just over half the primary heads are women and just under half are men. The document (issued by the NUT Salaries Department in September 1994) says that male teachers are 3.8 times more likely to be headteachers in the secondary sector and 4.45 times more likely to be headteacher in the primary sector.

[3] Shaw (1995, p.145) suggests that in primary schools, where most teachers are women, young learners may be exposed to 'ideals' of the 'good teacher', the 'good pupil' and the 'good parent' which project a female view and which may to some extent marginalise boys and generate anxiety about learning.

[4] Arnot *et al* (1996) showed an increase in gender monitoring in schools; this finding is confirmed by accounts of activities submitted by schools which indicate that they are both using evidence gathered in their own settings as a basis for planned intervention and also finding ways – sometimes with the support of local inspectors – of monitoring the impact of their interventions.

[5] Accounts of current approaches were sought via handouts distributed at conferences on gender, via personal contacts and via a letter in the *TES*. Responses came mainly from secondary schools.

Limitations on space in this report make it impossible to reproduce accounts of the reviews and interventions of individual schools, but the material so generously made available by schools and LEAs has informed the discussion in this chapter.

PART 5

RECOMMENDATIONS

Gender gaps in educational performance are a national problem. They may take different forms at different stages of pupils' school careers but in most schools gender patterns are a cause for concern. The size of the gap in performance in many schools suggests that they will need to launch several gender-related initiatives and to evaluate their impact on pupils both in the short- and medium-term.

The evidence on performance suggests that there are three areas where gaps arise:

- boys lag behind in early literacy skills and later on in English. The gap is evident as pupils enter school for the first time and remains sizeable throughout pupils' primary schooling and into the secondary stages.

- boys perform considerably less well than girls in GCSE examinations. A gap in the proportions of boys and girls securing five or more higher grade passes began to emerge in the late 1980s and has remained throughout the 1990s. Furthermore, girls have been making greater progress between the ages of 11 and 16 than have boys.

- girls continue to opt out of mathematics and science in the later stages of their educational careers. Although girls have begun to match boys in relation to entries and performance in mathematics and science at GCSE, many more boys still choose science or science-related subjects for further study. Boys still dominate science and technology at A-level and enter higher education to study these subjects in far larger numbers.

The overwhelming message from research is that there are no simple explanations for the gender gap in performance nor any simple solutions; in any one context several factors are likely to have an influence. For example, the ways in which pupils are grouped, the ways in which their work is assessed, the curricula they encounter, the teaching styles they experience, the role models they are offered, the expectations teachers have of boys and girls and the ways teachers reward and discipline them can all affect the size and nature of the gender gap.

Research also shows that what happens outside school can affect boys' and girls' performance in school. Factors affecting young people's attitudes and motivation include the nature of employment opportunities within the locality of the school, traditional expectations in the community about patterns of 'male' and 'female' employment and perceptions of the relevance of education to future lives and life chances. There is also evidence of a strong 'macho' peer culture that affects some boys' attitudes to schoolwork and homework.

Schools will be better able to address disparities in the performance of boys and girls if they know when and where they emerge. A careful analysis of data, mapping the development of male and female pupils, particularly their relative progress, including a breakdown of data by key pupil sub-groups, will enable schools to plan when and how to intervene. Schools should monitor pupils' progress regularly by gender, be sensitive to the particular patterns of achievement of their own pupils and understand how these relate to patterns in comparable schools and localities. They could also consider other areas where gender differences occur, such as behaviour, attendance and exclusion.

Within the framework of the national literacy initiatives, changes in teaching practice may be needed to counter boys' perception of literacy as a feminised subject. A reading and writing programme that engages the interest of all pupils will recognise the importance of balance, including the need for non-fiction and drama texts, and the potential contribution of book-reading clubs. The promotion of positive male and female role models in relation to the reading and enjoyment of books can have an impact on pupils' progress.

Differences in patterns of subject choice, especially post-16, are also a matter of concern and schools may wish to look at the strategies they use to break down gender stereotypes.

Where groups of boys and girls display an anti-achievement culture, schools should try to identify the source of their disaffection and develop appropriate strategies of intervention to remedy it.

Schools are already employing a number of strategies to narrow the gender gap, including:

- some single-sex groupings – for example, to enhance pupils' competence in particular subjects and to enable discussion of the way gender affects behaviour and learning;

- role modelling to challenge male and female stereotypes;

- mentoring of male and female pupils who need particular guidance by members of the senior management team, subject teachers, older pupils or outsiders, all of whom should be aware of the gender dimensions of performance.

Schools may want to consider developing their whole-school policies on gender to highlight achievement issues. All staff should be encouraged to see gender issues as matters of professional responsibility. Such a policy would require appropriate training and regular monitoring of its effectiveness, as well as support from management.

No matter who takes action, the central objective is to improve the academic performance of all pupils.

Abraham, J. (1995) *Divide and School: Gender and Class Dynamics in Comprehensive Education*. London, Falmer Press.

Acker, S. (1988) 'Teachers, gender and resistance', *British Journal of Sociology of Education*, 9, 3, 307–322.

Adkins, L. and Leonard, D. (1996) *The Family of Young People, Their Education and Post-16 Careers*. ESRC End of Award Report R000221179.

Alloway, N. and Gilbert, P. (1997) 'Boys and literacy: lessons from Australia', *Gender and Education*, 9, 1, 49–58.

Archer, J. and Macrae, M. (1991) 'Gender-perceptions of school subjects', *British Journal of Educational Psychology*, 61, 99–103.

Archer, J. and Lloyd, B. (1985) *Sex and Gender*. Cambridge, Cambridge University Press.

Arnot, M. (1982) 'Male hegemony, social class and women's education', *Journal of Education*, 164, 64–89.

Arnot, M., David, M., and Weiner, G. (1996) *Educational Reforms and Gender Equality in Schools*. Manchester, Equal Opportunities Commission.

Askew, S. (1989) 'Aggressive behaviour in boys: to what extent is it institutionalised?' In D. Tattum and D. Lane (eds) *Bullying in Schools*. Stoke-on-Trent, Trentham Books.

Askew, S. and Ross, C. (1988) *Boys Don't Cry. Boys and Sexism in Education*. Milton Keynes, Open University Press.

Bailey, V. (1992) *Student Non-Completion of BTEC Programmes and Awards*. Internal Report, London, BTEC.

Baird, J.A. (1996) *What's in a Name? Experiments with Blind-marking in A-level Examinations*. Guildford, AEB Report No.RAC/721.

Balding, J. *et al* (1996) *Bully Off: Young People That Fear Going to School*. Schools Health Education Unit, University of Exeter.

Ball. S.J. (1981) *Beachside Comprehensive. A Case-study of Secondary Schooling*. Cambridge, Cambridge University Press.

Basit, T.N. (1996) '"I'd hate to be just a housewife": career aspirations of British Muslim girls', *British Journal of Guidance and Counselling*, 24, 2, 227–242.

Bates, I. (1993) 'A job which is right for me?' In I. Bates and G. Riseborough (eds) *Youth and Inequality*. Milton Keynes, Open University Press.

Bates, I. and Riseborough, G. (eds) (1993) *Youth and Inequality*. Milton Keynes, Open University Press.

Belenky, M., Clinchy, B., Goldberger, N. and Tarule, J. (1986) *Women's Ways of Knowing: the Development of Self, Voice and Mind*. New York, Basic Books

Berends, M. (1995) 'Educational Stratification and Students' Social Bonding to School', *British Journal of Sociology of Education*, 16, 3, 327–352.

Besag, V.E. (1989) *Bullies and Victims in Schools*. Milton Keynes, Open University Press.

Bhavnani, R. (1994) *Black Women in the Labour Market: A Research Review.* Manchester, Equal Opportunities Commission.

Bishop, K., Bullock, K. and Martin, S. (1996) *Student Perceptions of the GCSE.* Paper presented at the ECER conference, Seville, September 1996.

Blackmore, J., Kenway, J., Willis, S. and Rennie, L. (1996) 'Feminist dilemmas: an Australian case study of a whole-school policy approach to gender reform', *Journal of Curriculum Studies,* 28, 3, 253–279.

Boaler, J. (1997) *Experiencing School Mathematics: Teaching Styles, Sex and Setting.* Milton Keynes, Open University Press.

Bolger, N. and Kellaghan, T. (1990) 'Method of measurement and gender differences in scholastic achievement', *Journal of Educational Measurement,* 27, 2, 165–174.

Bosker, R. and Dekkers, H. (1994) 'School differences in producing gender-related subject choices', *School Effectiveness and School Improvement,* 5, 2, 178–195.

Bowes, D. (1986) 'Single sex science teaching.' In D. Hustler, A. Cassidy and E. Cuff (eds) *Action Research in Classrooms and Schools.* London, Allen and Unwin.

Bradley, C. (1984) 'Sex bias in the evaluation of students', *British Journal of Social Psychology,* 23, 147–63.

Bray, R., Downes, P., Gardner, C., Hannan, G., and Parsons, N. (1997) *Can Boys Do Better?* Leicester, Secondary Heads Association.

Bridgwood, A. with Betteridge, J. (1989) *Equal Opportunities for Girls and Boys within TVEI.* Slough, NFER (an evaluation report prepared for the Training Agency).

Brown, L.M. and Gilligan, C. (1992) *Meeting at the Crossroads: Women's Psychology and Girls' Development.* Cambridge, Mass., Harvard University Press.

Brown, M. (1996) 'FIMS and SIMS: the first two IEA International Mathematics Surveys', *Assessment in Education,* 3, 2, 181–200.

Brown, P. (1987) *Schooling Ordinary Kids: Inequality, Unemployment, and the New Vocationalism.* London, Tavistock Publications.

Browne, N. and Ross, C. (1991) 'Girls' stuff, boys' stuff: young children talking and playing.' In N. Browne (ed.) *Science and Technology in the Early Years.* Milton Keynes, Open University Press.

Burnhill, P., Garner, C. and McPherson, A. (1990) 'Parental education, social class and entry to higher education 1976-1986.' *Journal of the Royal Statistical Society,* 153, 2, 233–248.

Burton, L., (1995) 'Moving towards a feminist epistemology of mathematics' in P. Rogers and G. Kaiser (eds) *Equity in Mathematics Education: Influences of Feminism and Culture.* Lewes, Falmer Press, pp.209–226.

Chaplain, R. (1996) 'Making a strategic withdrawal: disengagement and self-worth protection in male pupils.' In J. Rudduck, R. Chaplain, and G. Wallace (eds) *School Improvement. What Can Pupils Tell Us?* London, David Fulton.

Chaplain, R., Miles, S. and Rudduck, J. (1994) *Disengagement and Male Underachievement.* Cambridge, Homerton College (unpublished report of research undertaken for Derbyshire LEA).

Cheng, Y., Payne, J. and **Witherspoon, S.** (1995) *Science and Mathematics in Full-time Education After 16,* Youth Cohort Report No. 36. London, Department for Education and Employment.

Clark, A. and **Trafford, J.** (1995) 'Boys into modern languages: an investigation of the discrepancy in attitudes and performance between boys and girls in modern languages', *Gender and Education,* 7, 3, 315–325.

Clark, M. (1979) 'Anastasia is a normal developer because she is unique', *Oxford Review of Education,* 15, 3, 243–255.

Coffey, A.J. and **Acker, S.** (1991) '"Girlies on the Warpath": addressing gender in initial teacher education', *Gender and Education,* 3, 3, 249–261.

Colley, A., Comber, C. and **Hargreaves, D.J.** (1994) 'Gender effects in school subject preferences: a research note', *Educational Studies,* 20, 1, 13–18.

Comber, C., Hargreaves, D. J. and **Colley, A.** (1993) 'Girls, boys and technology in Music Education', *British Journal of Music Education,* 10, 123–134.

Comber, C. and Elwood, J. (1996) 'Gender differences in A-level Physics and English literature: is the future male or female?' *All-in success,* (Centre for the study of Comprehensive Schools) 7, 2, 20–21.

Committee on Women in Science, Engineering and Technology (1994) *The Rising Tide.* London, HMSO.

Commonwealth Schools Commission (1975) *Girls, School and Society,* Report by a Study Group to the Schools Commission, Canberra, Australian Government Publishing Service.

Commonwealth Schools Commission (1984) *Girls and Tomorrow, the Challenge for Schools,* Report of the Commonwealth Schools Commission Working Party on Education for Girls, Canberra, Australian Government Publishing Service.

Condor, S. (1989) 'Biting into the Future: social change and the social identity of women'. In S. Skevington and D. Baker (eds) *The Social Identity of Women.* London, Sage.

Connell, R. W. (1989) 'Cool Guys, Swots and Wimps: the interplay of masculinity and education', *Oxford Review of Education,* 15, 3, 291–303.

Connell, R.W. (1995) *Masculinities,* Cambridge, Polity Press.

Cooper, P., Upton, G., and **Smith, C.** (1991) 'Ethnic minority and gender distribution among staff and pupils in facilities for pupils with emotional and behavioural difficulties in England and Wales', *British Journal of Sociology of Education,* 12, 1, 77–93.

Cresswell, M.J. (1990) 'Gender effects in GCSE - some initial analyses', paper prepared for a Nuffield Assessment Seminar at the University of London Institute of Education, June 1990.

Crozier, G. and **Menter, I.** (1993) 'The Heart of the Matter? Student teachers' experiences in school.' In I.S. Blatchford (ed.) *Race, Gender and the Education of Teachers.* Milton Keynes, Open University Press.

Crump, S.J. (1990) 'Gender and curriculum: power and being female', *British Journal of Sociology of Education,* 11, 4, 365–385.

Cullingford, C. (1993) 'Children's views on gender issues in school', *British Educational Research Journal*, 19, 5, 555–563.

Daly, P. (1995) 'Science course participation and science achievement in single sex and co-educational schools', *Evaluation and Research in Education*, 9, 2, 91–98.

Daly, P. (1996) 'The effects of single-sex and co-educational secondary schooling on girls' achievement' *Research Papers in Education*, 11, 3, 289–306.

Daly, P. and Shuttleworth, I. (1995) 'Public examination entry and attainment in mathematics in single-sex and co-educational schools', paper presented to the European Conference on Educational Research, Bath, England.

Daly, P., Ainley, J. and Robinson, L. (1996) 'The influence of single-sex secondary schooling on choice of science courses', paper presented to the Annual Conference of the American Educational Research Association, New York.

Daniels, H., Hey, V., Leonard, D. and Smith, M. (1994) 'Gendered practice in special educational needs.' In L. Dawtrey *et al* (eds) *Equality and Inequality in Education Policy*. Clevedon, Multilingual Matters.

Daniels, H., Hey, V., Leonard, D. and Smith, M. (1996) *Gender and Special Needs Provision in Mainstream Schooling*. ESRC End of Award Report R000235059.

Dart, B. and Clarke, J. (1988) 'Sexism in schools: a new look', *Educational Review*, 40, 41–49.

David, M., West, A. and Ribbens, J. (1994) *Mothers' Intuition? Choosing Secondary Schools*. Lewes, Falmer Press.

Davie, R., Butler, N. and Goldstein, H. (1972) *From Birth to Seven*. London, Longman.

Davies, B. (1989) *Frogs and Snails and Feminist Tales*. Sydney, Allen and Unwin.

Davies, B. (1993) *Shards of Glass*. Sydney, Allen and Unwin.

Davies, L. (1990) *Equity and Efficiency? School Management in an International Context*. Lewes, Falmer Press.

Deem, R. (ed.) (1984) *Co-education Reconsidered*. Milton Keynes, Open University Press.

Delamont, S. (1990) *Sex Roles and the School*. London, Methuen.

Department of Education and Science (1988a) *Science at Age 11 - A Review of APU Findings*. London, HMSO.

Department of Education and Science (1988b) *Science at Age 15 - A Review of APU Findings*. London, HMSO.

Department of Education and Science (1989) *Science at Age 13 - A Review of APU Findings*. London, HMSO.

DfEE (1995) *Participation in Education and Training by 16-18 Year Olds in England: 1984/85 to 1994/95*. London, Department for Education and Employment.

DfEE (1996a) *Results from the 1995 National Curriculum Assessments of Seven-Year-Olds in England*. London, Department for Education and Employment.

DfEE (1996b) *Results from the 1995 National Curriculum Assessments of Eleven-Year-Olds in England*. London, Department for Education and Employment.

DfEE (1996c) *Results from the 1995 National Curriculum Assessments of Fourteen-Year-Olds in England*. London, Department for Education and Employment.

DfEE (1996d) *GCSE and GCE A/AS Level Performance of Candidates Attempting Two or More GCE A/AS Levels in 1994/95*, Statistical Bulletin, 2/96.

Drew, D. and Gray, J. (1990) 'The fifth year examination achievements of Black young people in England and Wales', *Educational Research*, 32, 3, 107–117.

Drew, D., Gray, J. and Sime, N. (1992) *Against the Odds: The Education and Labour Market Experiences of Black Young People*, Sheffield: Department of Employment Research and Development Series, no. 68.

Drew, D., Gray, J. and Sporton, D. (1997) Ethnic differences in the educational participation of 16-19 year olds, in V. Karn (ed.) *Employment, Education and Housing Amongst Ethnic Minorities in Britain: Evidence from the 1991 Census*, Volume 3, London, HMSO for Office of Population Censuses and Surveys.

Dweck, C.S. (1986) 'Motivational processes affecting learning', *American Psychologist*, 41, 1041–1048.

Dweck, C.S., Davidson, W., Nelson, S. and Enna, B. (1978) Sex Differences in Learned Helplessness II. The contingencies of evaluative feedback in the classroom. III An experimental analysis, *Departmental Psychology*, 124, 268–276.

Edwards, S. and Lyons, G. (1996) 'It's grim up North for female high-flyers', *Times Educational Supplement*, 10 May.

Elwood, J. (1995) 'Undermining gender stereotypes: examination and coursework performance in the UK at 16', *Assessment in Education*. 2, 3, 283–303.

Elwood, J. and Comber, C. (1996) *Gender Differences in Examinations at 18+: Final Report*. London, London University Institute of Education.

Epstein, D. (1997) 'Boyz' Own Stories: masculinities and schedules in schools', *Gender and Education*, 9, 1, 105–116.

Equal Opportunities Commission, (1995a) *The Life Cycle of Inequality: Women and Men in Britain 1995*. Manchester, EOC.

Equal Opportunities Commission, (1995b) *Challenging Inequalities Between Men and Women:* Annual Report. Manchester, EOC.

Felstead, A., Goodwin, J. and Green, F. (1995) *Measuring Up to the National Training Targets: Women's Attainment of Vocational Qualifications*. Research Report. Leicester, Centre for Labour Market Studies, University of Leicester.

Ford, J., Mongon, D. and Whelan, M. (1982) *Special Education and Social Control*. London, Routledge and Kegan Paul.

Foxman, D., Ruddock, G., Joffe, L., Mason, K., Mitchell, P. and Sexton, B. (1985) *A Review of Monitoring in Mathematics Performance 1978-1982, Part 1 and Part 2*. London, DES.

Frazer, E. (1989) 'Feminist talk and talking about feminism: teenage girls' discourses of gender', *Oxford Review of Education*, 15, 3, 281–290.

Furlong, V.J. (1986) 'Schools and the structure of female occupational aspirations', *British Journal of Sociology of Education*, 7, 4, 367–376.

Gardiner, H. (1983) *Frames of Mind: the Theory of Multiple Intelligences*. New York, Basic Books.

Garratt, L. (1986) 'Gender differences in relation to science choice at A-level', *Educational Review*, 38, 1, 67–77.

Gaskell, J. (1992) *Gender Matters from School to Work*. Milton Keynes, Open University Press.

Gill, J. (1988) *Which Way to School? A Review of the Evidence on the Single-sex Versus Co-education Debate*. Canberra, Commonwealth Schools Commission.

Gillborn D. (1990) *'Race', Ethnicity and Education: Teaching and Learning in Multi-ethnic Schools*. London, Unwin Hyman.

Gillborn, D. (1997) 'Young, black and failed by school: the market, education reform and black students'. *International Journal of Inclusive Education*, 1, 1, 65–87.

Gillborn, D. and **Gipps, C.** (1996) *Recent Research on the Achievements of Ethnic Minority Pupils*, OFSTED Reviews of Research. London, HMSO.

Gilligan, C. (1982) *In a Different Voice: Psychological Theory and Women's Development*. Cambridge, Mass., Harvard University Press.

Gipps, C. and **Murphy, P.** (1994) *A Fair Test? Assessment, Achievement and Equity*. Milton Keynes, Open University Press.

Goddard-Spear, M. (1983) 'Sex bias in science teachers' ratings of work.' In *Contributions to the Second GASAT Conference*, Oslo.

Goddard-Spear, M. (1985) 'Teachers' attitudes towards girls and technology.' In J. Whyte, R. Deem, L. Kant and M. Cruickshank (eds) *Girl Friendly Schooling*. London, Methuen.

Golombok, S. and **Fivush, R.** (1994) *Gender Development*. Cambridge, Cambridge University Press.

Gorman, T., White, J., Brooks, G. and **English, F.** (1991) *Assessment Matters No. 4: Language for Learning*. London, SEAC.

Goulding, M. (1995) 'GCSE coursework in mathematics: teachers' perspectives and the performance of girls', *Evaluation and Research in Education*, 9, 3, 111–19.

Graham, J. (1994) 'Gender Differences and GCSE results'. Centre for Successful Schools, Keele University, unpublished research report.

Gray, J., Jesson, D. and **Sime, N.** (1992) 'The "discouraged worker" revisited: post-16 participation south of the border', *Sociology*, 26, 3, 493–505.

Gray, J., Jesson, D. and **Tranmer, M.** (1993) *Boosting Post-16 Participation: A Study of Key Factors*, Sheffield: Department of Employment Research and Development Series No. 20.

Gray, J. and **Wilcox, B.** (1995) *'Good School, Bad School': Evaluating Performance and Encouraging Improvement*. Milton Keynes, Open University Press.

Griffin, C. (1989) '"I'm not a Women's Libber but…." Feminism, Consciousness and Identity.' In S. Skevington and D. Baker (eds) *The Social Identity of Women*, London, Sage.

Griffin. C. (1989) *Typical Girls? Young Women from School to the Job Market*. London, Routledge and Kegan Paul.

Halpern, D.F. (1992) *Sex Differences in Cognitive Abilities.* New Jersey, Hillsdale Publishers (2nd ed.).

Hannan, D., Smyth, E., McCullagh, J., O'Leary, R. and McMahon, D. (1996) *Co-education and Gender Equality: Examination Performance, Stress and Personal Development.* Dublin, Oak Tree Press.

Hansford, B.C. and Hattie, J.A. (1982) 'The Relationship Between Self and Achievement/Performance Measures', *Review of Educational Research,* 52, 1, 123–142.

Hargreaves, D.H. (1967) *Social Relations in a Secondary School,* London, Routledge and Kegan Paul.

Harris, S., Nixon, J. and Rudduck, J. (1993) 'Schoolwork, homework and gender', *Gender and Education,* 3, 3–14.

Harvey, T.J. (1985) 'Science in single sex and mixed teaching groups', *Educational Research,* 27, 3, 179–182.

Harvey, T.J. and Stables, A. (1986) 'Gender differences in attitudes to science for third year pupils: an argument for single-sex groups in mixed schools', *Research in Science and Technological Education,* 4, 2, 163–169.

Henshaw, A., Kelly, J. and Gratton, C. (1992) 'Skipping for Girls: children's perceptions of gender roles and gender preferences', *Educational Research,* 34, 2, 229–235.

Hill, J. (1994) 'The Paradox of Gender: Sex stereotyping within statementing procedures', *British Educational Research Journal,* 20, 3, 345–354.

Hill, P.W., Holmes-Smith, P. and Rowe, K.J. (1993) *School and Teacher Effectiveness in Victoria: Key findings from Phase 1 of the Victoria Quality Schools Project.* Melbourne, Centre for Applied Educational Research, University of Melbourne.

Hodgeon, J. (1988) *A Woman's World? A Report on a Project in Cleveland Nurseries on Sex Differentiation in the Early Years.* Unpublished report sponsored jointly by Cleveland Education Committee and the EOC.

Holland, J., Ramazanogei, C. and Sharpe, S. (1993) *Wimp or Gladiator? Contradictions in Acquiring Masculine Sexuality.* London, Tufnell Press.

Howe, C. (1997) *Gender and Classroom Interaction: a research review,* Edinburgh, SCRE.

Hughes, G. (1996) 'Implications of Employment Trends in Ireland, the Netherlands and the United Kingdom for the Occupations Today's Students will Enter.' Paper for European Union Conference on Gender Equality for 2000 and Beyond.

Huston, A. (1985) 'The development of sex-typing: themes from recent research', *Developmental Review,* 5, 1–17.

Imsen, G. (1996) 'Gender Equality as an Educational Objective. Some Results from a National Evaluation Study in Norway.' Paper presented at European Conference on Educational Research, University of Seville, Spain. (Source: Department of Education, Norwegian University of Science and Technology, Trondheim.)

ILEA (1984) *Improving Secondary Schools,* (The Hargreaves Report). London, Inner London Education Authority.

Jenkins, R. (1983) *Working-Class Youth Life-Styles in Belfast.* London, Routledge and Kegan Paul.

Jesson, D. (1998) 'Making sense of gender differences in examination results.' In A. Clark and E. Millard (eds) *Gender in the Secondary Curriculum: Balancing the Books.* London, Routledge.

Joffe, L. and Foxman, D. (1988) *Attitudes and Gender Differences.* Slough, NFER-Nelson.

Johnson, S. (1996) 'The contribution of large-scale assessment programmes to research on gender differences', *Educational Research and Evaluation*, 2, 1, 25–49.

Jones, M. and Gerig, T. (1994). 'Silent sixth-grade students: characteristics, achievement, and teacher expectations', *The Elementary School Journal*, 95, 169–182.

Keise, C. (1992) *Sugar and Spice. Bullying in Single-Sex Schools.* Stoke-on-Trent, Trentham Books.

Kelly E. and Cohen, T. (1988) *Racism in Schools - New Research Evidence.* Stoke-on-Trent, Trentham Books

Kelly, A. (1988) 'Gender differences in teacher-pupil interaction: a meta-analytic review', *Research in Education*, 39, 1–23.

Kelly, A. (1989) '"When I Grow Up I Want to Be ...": A Longitudinal Study of the Development of Career Preferences', *British Journal of Guidance and Counselling*, 17, 2, 179–200.

Kenway, J. (1995) 'Masculinities in schools; under siege, on the defensive and under reconstruction?' *Discourse: Studies in the Cultural Politics of Education*, 16, 1, 59–79.

Kenway, J. and Willis, S. (eds) (1990) *Hearts and Minds: Self Esteem and the Schooling of Girls.* Lewes, Falmer Press.

Kessler, S. *et al* (1987) 'Gender relations in secondary schooling.' In M. Arnot, and G. Weiner (eds) *Gender and the Politics of Schooling.* London, Hutchinson.

Keys, W., Harris, S. and Fernandes, C. (1996) *Third International Study of Maths and Science.* Slough, NFER.

Kimbell, R., Stables, K., Wheeler, T., Wosniak, A. and Kelly, V. (1991) *The Assessment of Performance in Design and Technology.* London, School Examinations and Assessment Council.

Kruse, A. (1992) '"... We have learnt not just to sit back, twiddle our thumbs and let them all take over." Single-sex settings and the development of a pedagogy for girls and a pedagogy for boys in Danish Schools', *Gender and Education*, 4, 1–2, 81-103.

Lamb, S. (1996) 'Gender differences in mathematics participation in Australian schools: some relationships with social class and school policy', *British Educational Research Journal*, 22, 2, 223–241.

Lee, V. and Bryk, A. (1986) 'Effects of single-sex secondary schools on student achievement and attitudes', *Journal of Educational Psychology*, 78, 5, 381–395.

Lees, S. (1986) *Losing Out: Sexuality and Adolescent Girls.* London, Hutchinson.

Lees, S. (1993) *Sugar and Spice: Sexuality and Adolescent Girls,* London, Penguin.

Lees, S. (1998) 'Will boys be left on the shelf?' In G. Jagger and C. Wright (eds) *Changing Family Values. Difference, diversity and the decline of the male order.* London, Routledge.

Lightbody, P. and Durndell, A. (1996) 'Gendered career choice: is sex stereotyping the cause or the consequence?' *Educational Studies*, 22, 2, 133–146.

Lightbody, P., Siann, G., Stocks, R. and Walsh, D. (1996) 'Motivation and Attribution at Secondary School: the role of gender', *Educational Studies*, 22, 1, 13–25.

Lloyd, B. and Duveen, G. (1992) *Gender Identities and Education. The Impact of Starting School*. London, Harvester Wheatsheaf.

Lucey, H. and Walkerdine, V. (1996) 'Transitions to Womanhood: Constructions of Success and Failure for Middle and Working Class Young Women', Paper presented at British Youth Research: The New Agenda, Glasgow University, January 1996.

Mac an Ghaill, M. (1988) *Young, Gifted and Black*. Milton Keynes, Open University Press.

Mac an Ghaill, M. (1994) *The Making of Men: Masculinities, Sexualities and Schooling*. Milton Keynes, Open University Press.

Mac an Ghaill, M. (ed.) (1996) *Understanding Masculinities*. Milton Keynes, Open University Press.

McClaren, A. (1996) 'Coercive Invitations: how young women in school make sense of mothering and waged labour', *British Journal of Sociology of Education*, 17, 3, 279–298.

Maccoby, E.E. and Jacklin, C.N. (1974) *The Psychology of Sex Differences*. London, Oxford University Press.

MacLeod, M. and Morris, S. (1996) *Why Me? Children Talking to Childline about Bullying*. London, Childline.

Mann, C. (1997) *Finding a Favourable Front; the Celebration of the Family and Working Class Girls' Educational Achievement*. Cambridge, Department of Education, Cambridge University. (unpublished doctoral thesis).

Marsh, H. (1989) 'Effects of attending single-sex and co-educational high schools on achievement, attitudes, behaviours and sex differences', *Journal of Educational Psychology*, 81, 1, 70–85.

Martinez, L. (1994) 'Boyswork - whose work?', *REDRESS*, 3–12 (November).

Martino, W. (1994) 'Masculinity and learning: exploring boys' underachievement and under-representation in subject English', *Interpretations*, 27, 2, 22–56.

McRobbie, A. (1978) 'Working class girls and the culture of femininity.' In Women's Studies Group (eds), *Women Take Issue*. London, Hutchinson.

Measor, L., Tuffin, C. and Fry, K. (1996) 'Gender and sex education: a study of adolescent responses', *Gender and Education*, 8, 3, 275–288.

Menter, I. (1989) 'Teaching Practice Stasis: racism, sexism and school experience in initial teacher education', *British Journal of Sociology of Education*, 10, 4, 459–473.

Millard, E. (1996) 'Some thoughts on why boys don't choose to read in school' (unpublished paper), University of Sheffield.

Millen, D., Rudduck, J., and Gray, J. (1994) *The NETTS School Commitment Project: A Review*. Cambridge, Eastern Region Government Department NETTS Project.

Millman, V. and Weiner, G. (1987) 'Engendering equal opportunities: the case of TVEI.' In D. Gleeson (ed.) *TVEI and Secondary Education: A Critical Appraisal.* Milton Keynes, Open University Press.

Mirza, H.S. (1992) *Young, Female and Black.* London, Routledge.

Mortimore, P., Sammons, P., Stoll, L., Lewis, D. and Ecob, R. (1988) *School Matters: The Junior School Years.* Wells, Open Books.

Murphy, R. (1982) 'Sex differences in objective test performance', *British Journal of Educational Psychology,* 52, 213–19.

National Advisory Council for Education and Training Targets (1994) *Report on Progress.* London, NACETT.

National Advisory Council for Education and Training Targets (1995) *Developing Skills for a Successful Future,* London, NACETT.

National Commission on Education (1993) *Learning to Succeed: A Radical Look at Education Today and a Strategy for the Future,* Report of the Paul Hamlyn Foundation National Commission on Education, London, Heinemann.

North London TEC/Chief Executives Network (1996) *Disaffection and Non-Participation in Education, Training and Employment by Individuals Aged 18-20,* London, DfEE.

Nuttall, D., Goldstein, H., Prosser, R. and Rasbash, J. (1989) 'Differential school effectiveness', *International Journal of Educational Research,* 13, 769–776.

Oakley, A. (1996) 'Gender Matters: Man the Hunter.' In H. Roberts and D. Sachdev (eds) *Young People's Social Attitudes: Having Their Say.* Basildon, Barnardos.

OECD (1995) *Education at a Glance.* Paris, OECD.

OFSTED (1993) *Boys and English.* London.

OFSTED (1996) *Exclusions from Secondary Schools.* London.

OFSTED/EOC (1996) *The Gender Divide: Performance Differences Between Boys and Girls at School.* London, HMSO.

OFSTED (1997) *The Annual Report of Her Majesty's Chief Inspector of Schools: Standards and Quality in Education 1995/96.* London, HMSO.

Orr, P. (1985) 'Sex bias in schools: national perspectives.' In J. Whyte, R. Deem, L. Kant., and M. Cruickshank, (eds) *Girl Friendly Schooling.* London, Methuen.

Paechter, C. and Head, J. (1996) 'Gender identity, status and the body: life in a marginal subject', *Gender and Education,* 8, 1, 21–29.

Parsons, C. (1995) *Final Report to the Department for Education: National survey of local authorities' policies and procedures for the identification of, and provision for, children who are out of school by reason of exclusion or otherwise,* London, DfEE.

Payne, J. (1995) *Routes Beyond Compulsory Schooling,* Youth Cohort Report No.31. Sheffield, Department of Employment.

Pidgeon, S. (1993) 'Learning Reading and Learning Gender'. In M. Barrs and S. Pidgeon (eds) *Reading the Difference.* London, Centre for Language in Primary Education.

Pitts, J. and Smith, P. (1995) *Preventing School Bullying,* Police Research Group, Crime Detection and Prevention Series, Paper 63.

Poole, M. and Issacs, D. (1993) 'The gender agenda in teacher education', *British Journal of Education*, 14, 3, 275–281.

Powell, R. (1979) 'Sex differences and language learning: a review of the evidence', *Audio-Visual Journal*, 17, 19–24.

Powney, J. (1996) *Gender and Attainment: A Review*. Edinburgh, Scottish Council for Research in Education.

Punter, A. and Burchell, H. (1996) 'Gender issues in GCSE English assessment', *British Journal of Curriculum and Assessment*, 6, 2, 20–23.

Quicke, J. (1995) 'Gender and GCSE results: what schools are doing', paper presented at the British Educational Research Association Annual Conference, University of Bath.

Raffe, D. and Willms, J.D. (1989) 'Schooling the discouraged worker: local-labour-market effects on educational participation', *Sociology*, 23, 4, 559–581.

Reay, D. (1990) 'Working with boys', *Gender and Education*, 2, 3, 269–282.

Rennie, L.J. and Parker, L.H. (1987) 'Detecting and accounting for gender differences in mixed-sex and single-sex groupings in science lessons', *Educational Review*, 39, 1, 65–73.

Renshaw, P. (1990) 'Self-esteem research and equity programs'. In J. Kenway and S. Willis (eds) *Hearts and Minds*. Lewes, Falmer Press.

Reynolds, D. and Farrell, S. (1996) *Worlds Apart? A Review of International Surveys of Educational Achievement Involving England*. OFSTED Reviews of Research. London, HMSO.

Riddell, S. (1996) 'Gender and Special Educational Needs.' In G. Lloyd (ed.) *Knitting Progress Unsatisfactory. Gender and Special Issues in Education*. Edinburgh, Moray House Publications.

Riddell, S., Brown, S. and Duffield, J. (1994) 'Parental power and special educational needs: the case of specific learning difficulties', *British Educational Research Journal*, 20, 3, 327–345.

Riordan, C. (1990) *Girls and Boys in School: Together or Separate?* New York, Teachers College Press.

Roker, D. (1993) 'Gaining the edge: girls at a private school.' In I. Bates and G. Riseborough (eds) *Youth and Inequality*. Milton Keynes, Open University Press.

Rowe, K.J. (1988) 'Single-sex and mixed-sex classes: the effects of class type on student achievement, confidence and participation in mathematics', *Australian Journal of Education*, 32, 2, 180–202.

Rudduck, J. (1994) *Developing a Gender Policy in Secondary Schools*. Milton Keynes, Open University Press.

Rutter, M. (1975) *Helping Troubled Children*. London, Penguin (1987 edition).

Salisbury, J. and Jackson, D. (1996) *Challenging Macho Values: Practical Ways of Working with Adolescent Boys*. Lewes, Falmer Press.

Sammons, P. (1995) 'Gender, ethnic and socio-economic differences in attainment and progress', *British Educational Research Journal*, 21, 4, 465–485.

Sammons, P. (1996) 'Complexities in the judgment of school effectiveness', *Educational Research and Evaluation*, 2, 2, 113–149.

Sammons, P., Nuttall, D., Cuttance, P. and Thomas, S. (1995) 'Continuity of school effects: a longitudinal analysis of primary and secondary school effects on GCSE performance', *School Effectiveness and School Improvement*, 6, 4, 285–307.

Schmitt, A.P., Mazzeo, J. and Bleistein, C. (1991) *Are gender differences between placement multiple-choice and constructed response sections a function of multiple-choice DIF?* Princeton, NJ, Educational Testing Service.

Senior Secondary Assessment Board of South Australia (SSABSA) (1993) *Gender Equity in Senior Secondary School Assessment Project: Final Report*. South Australia, SSABSA.

Sewell, T. (1997) *Black Masculinities and Schooling: How Black Boys Survive Modern Schooling*. London, Trentham Books.

Sharpe, S. (1992) *Just Like A Girl*. London, Penguin (1st ed.)

Sharpe, S. (1994) *Just Like A Girl: How Girls Learn to be Women*. London, Penguin. (2nd ed.)

Shaw, J. (1995) *Education, Gender and Anxiety*. London, Taylor and Francis.

Skaalvik, E. M.(1986) 'Academic achievement, self-esteem and valuing of the school - some sex differences', *British Journal of Educational Psychology*, 53, 299–306.

Skelton, C. (1989) 'And so the wheel turns...gender and initial teacher education.' In C. Skelton (ed.) *Whatever Happens to Little Women?* Milton Keynes, Open University Press.

Skeggs B. (1988) 'Gender reproduction and further education: domestic apprenticeships', *British Journal of Sociology of Education*, 9, 2, 131–149.

Smith, S. (1984) 'Single-sex setting.' In R. Deem (ed.) *Co-Education Reconsidered*, Milton Keynes, Open University Press.

Smithers, A. and Robinson, P. (1995) *Co-Educational and Single-Sex Schooling*. University of Manchester: Centre for Education and Employment Research.

Stables, A. and Stables, S. (1995) 'Gender differences in students' approaches to A-level subject choices and perceptions of A-level subjects: a study of first-year A-level students in a tertiary college', *Educational Research*, 37, 1, 39–51.

Stables, A. and Winkeley, F. (1996) 'Pupil Approaches to Subject Option Choices.' Paper presented at the European Conference on Educational Research held at the University of Seville, Spain.

Steedman, J. (1985) *Examination Results in Mixed and Single-Sex Schools: Findings from the National Child Development Study*. Manchester, Equal Opportunities Commission.

Stephenson, P. and Smith, D. (1989) 'Bullying in the Junior School.' In D. Tattum and D. Lane (eds) *Bullying in Schools*. Stoke-on-Trent, Trentham Books.

Stobart, G., Elwood, J. and Quinlan, M. (1992a) 'Gender bias in Examinations: how equal are the opportunities?' *British Educational Research Journal*, 18, 3, 261–276.

Stobart, G., White, J., Elwood, J., Hayden, M. and Mason, K. (1992b) *Differential Performance at 16+: English and Mathematics*. London, HMSO.

Swann, J. (1992) *Girls, Boys and Language*. Oxford, Blackwell.

Taber, K.S. (1992) 'Girls' interactions with teachers in mixed physics classes - results of classroom observation', *International Journal of Science Education*, 14, 163–180.

Taylor, M.T. and Mardle, G.D. (1986) 'Pupils' attitudes towards gender roles', *Educational Research*, 28, 3, 202–9.

Thomas, S., Pan, H. and Goldstein, H. (1994) *Report on an Analysis of 1992 Examination Results.* London, AMA and London University Institute of Education.

Tomlinson, S. (1982) *The Sociology of Special Education.* London, Routledge and Kegan Paul.

Tomlinson, S. (1988) 'Why Johnny can't read: critical theory and special education', *European Journal of Special Needs Education*, 3, 1, 45–48.

Walkerdine, V. (1989) *Counting Girls Out.* London, Virago.

Walkerdine, V. (1990) *Schoolgirl Fictions.* London, Verso.

Walkerdine, V., Melody, J. and Lucey, H. (1996) *Project 4:21: Transition to Womanhood.* ESRC End of Award Report, R000234680.

Wallace, C. (1987) 'From girls and boys to women and men: the social reproduction of gender.' In M. Arnot, and G. Weiner (eds) *Gender and the Politics of Schooling.* London, Hutchinson.

Warrington, M. and Younger, M. (1995) 'I want it done now, before *Neighbours* and *Home and Away* start.' In R. Chaplain, J. Rudduck, and G. Wallace (eds) *School Improvement: What Can Pupils Tell Us?* London, David Fulton.

Weiner, G. and Arnot, M. (1987) 'Teachers and Gender Politics.' In M. Arnot and G. Weiner (eds) *Gender and the Politics of Schooling.* London, Hutchinson.

White, J. (1986) 'The writing on the wall: beginning or end of a girl's career?' *Women's Studies International Forum*, 9, 5, 561–574.

Whitney, I. and Smith, P.K. (1993) 'A survey of the nature and extent of bullying in junior/middle and secondary schools', *Educational Research*, 35, 1, 3–25.

Williams, K. *et al* (1996) 'Association of common health symptoms with bullying in primary school children', *British Medical Journal*, 313, 6 July, 17–19.

Wilcox, B., Wilcox, J. and Gray, J. (1996) 'Getting into the pack: school improvement in context', paper presented to the Annual Conference of the British Educational Research Association held at Lancaster University.

Willis, P. (1977) *Learning to Labour.* Farnborough, Saxon House.

Willis, P. (1985) *Youth Unemployment and the New Poverty. A Summary of Local Authority Review and Framework for Policy Development on Youth and Youth Unemployment.* Wolverhampton, Wolverhampton Local Authority.

Wilkinson, H. (1994) *No Turning Back: Generations and the Genderquake.* London, Demos.

Wilkinson, H. and Mulgan, G. (1995) *Freedom's Children: Work, Relationships and Politics for 18-34 year olds in Britain Today.* London, Demos.

Witkin, H.A., Dyk, R.B., Faterson, H.F., Goodenough, D.G. and Karp, S.A. (1962) *Psychological Differentiation.* New York, Wiley.

Wolpe, A. (1989) *Within School Walls.*
London, Routledge.

Wright, C. (1987) 'The relations between
teachers and Afro-Caribbean pupils:
observing a multiracial classroom.' In G.
Weiner and M. Arnot (eds) *Gender Under
Scrutiny.* London, Hutchinson.

Wright, C. (1986) 'School processes - an
ethnographic study.' In J. Eggleston *et al*
(eds) *Education for Some: the Educational
and Vocational Experiences of 15-18 year old
Members of Minority Ethnic Groups.*
London, Routledge.

Wright, C. (1992) *Race Relations in
Primary Schools.* London, David Fulton.

Wylie, R.C. (1979) *The Self Concept:* Vol.2,
Lincoln, Nebraska, University of Nebraska
Press.

Yates, L. (1993) *The Education of Girls:
Research and the Question of Gender.*
Australian Council for Educational
Research.

Younger, M. & **Warrington, M.** (1996)
'Differential achievement of girls and boys
at GCSE: some observations from the
perspective of one school', *British Journal
of Sociology of Education.* 17, 3, 299–313.

Printed in the United Kingdom for The Stationery Office
J53454 C25 7/98 19585